SIDELINED

From FSU to Prison and the
Return to the Game of Life

Maurice Harris

as told to

Robert L Congress

SIDELINED

Copyright © 2022 Maurice Harris

ISBN: 978-0-692-15277-5

Published by

Candy Publishing

Printed in the United States of America

Editor
Bakeba C. Raines/Edits by Bakeba

Cover Photo Credit
Cameron Meller/NoleDigest.com

Interior Photos
247SPORTS
Seminoles.com

DEDICATION

My Everything

I dedicate this book to ALL ONE LOVE
(After Limiting Limits Oneness Never Ends Living Over Various
Enemies)

This defines how I and most are molded into our perfectly
flawed selves. That we are touched and moved by things
that are miles away, that we may have never touched but is
constantly in our immediate proximity. To be more
specific, my dedication to ALL negative and positive,
absent and present people and things that ARE. My
dedication is a total appreciation of LIFE and its necessary
deaths. Without one there is not another so there is an
infinite and finite that can't be expressed, and confusion
that's obviously clear.

Thanks for Everything and Nothing

SIDELINED

CONTENTS

The Seriousness of Being Sidelined

I have been sidelined many times during my life and for various amounts of time. Putting my all into something, being depended on, and not wanting to let myself or those closest to me down, made being sidelined more difficult. Being sidelined quite often results in having mental, physical, and emotional limitations that impact your ability to perform at an optimal level, making even the most menial task difficult to complete.

My entire football career, ages six through twenty, was an accumulation of bad hits, nicks, bruises, and stingers. The hits finally took their toll in college.

Who could understand the rise and fall of a college student-athlete? Those who could maybe understand were just as sad as me or just didn't want to talk about it. I was sidelined, with no one around that could relate to my circumstances. I decided to end the game of football because of the memory of not having feelings in my legs, a small glimpse of becoming paralyzed because of football. I was never fully content with my decision and always felt as if I was a failure, a quitter. I spiraled into many bad habits and was sentenced to eight years in prison because of it.

My most recent time being sidelined is when I was in the Virgin Islands working for a company called Florida Welding, doing steel fabrication and erection.

I have chosen, as I wish most would do, to be the decision-maker in my own life: Become Your Most Valuable Person.

March 18, 2017

To: Todd Stroud

From: Maurice Harris

Subject: Letter of apology

Dear Coach Stroud (Todd),

I am writing to apologize for my ignorance and immaturity; it took me coming to prison to write it down on paper. I now look back and see the many opportunities you gave me through my many emotions and endless hope for the best. Unfortunately, all you saw of me was the mask I had built up. The smile was so no one would see my true pain and misery. It's hard looking back and seeing the many glimpses of my past and reconciling those memories to the person I am today. Not only were you an authoritative figure in my life, but you were also and still are, the leading example and mentor I used to mold myself into the man I've become today. In humility and with the utmost respect, I hope you will one day accept my most heartfelt sincere apology.

One Absolute – formally known as Maurice "Smiley" Harris

1

THE DAY AFTER

May 6, 2011, one day after the rape of my girlfriend Whitney, I remember being in bed and asking myself, how could I have possibly violated the person I professed to care so deeply for? In my mind, I could not help but wonder if she was okay. Feeling disgusted and ashamed, all I thought about was calling her. She was obviously feeling something also because she called me saying she was dropping the charges. I wasn't surprised, but I was relieved. Maybe she realized that my actions, although completely unacceptable, were not meant to harm her in any way. She also mentioned that I needed a lawyer. She eventually found an attorney for me who charged $5,000 but he said

I didn't have a case. I didn't have the money then, but looking back, you won't find a lawyer these days for that amount of money.

All I wanted to do was to see Whitney. In my mind, at the time, I was convinced that seeing her would somehow make everything okay, so I picked up the phone and called her. Whitney answered. What I didn't know was our conversation was being secretly recorded and shared with the investigating police officer involved with the rape charges filed against me on behalf of the State of Florida. Initially, during our conversation, it was clear to me that she was extremely uneasy about talking to me. She told me that if I went to counseling the charges would be dropped, but my only objective at the time was seeing her. I asked if I could come and see her. She responded by saying no, and that she was getting ready to attend a pool party. The conversation ended with her telling me we would talk later.

That same day, I spoke with my mother. I wanted to know her thoughts regarding my wanting to drive from Albany, Georgia to Tallahassee, Florida to see Whitney. My mother told me it wasn't a good idea and I shouldn't go. It was not the answer I wanted to hear. I needed to see Whitney. It was my way of controlling the situation and manipulating my relationship with Whitney; something I had become quite accustomed to doing. And not even my mother was going to stop me.

The next day, was a typical sunny summer day in Albany. I had just purchased a new car and putting it on the road, helped justify my misguided need to see her even more. I didn't realize I was placing myself on a path that would ultimately change the course of my life– thrusting me into a series of unforeseen nightmares.

Before I got on the road, I started drinking a bottle of cheap vodka. I guess tipping the bottle back was my way of dealing with or numbing the emotional guilt I was feeling on the inside.

"Once the police arrived, I was consumed with embarrassment, but a deep feeling of relief shadowed my shame. I felt rescued from life and all the hoping, wishing, and working for something I didn't have a clue how to find. The police arrived and I sat in her p a t r o l car while being handcuffed. I remember the handcuffs being really uncomfortable. I silently questioned my actions and wondered what was next for me".

With the bottle of liquor on the seat beside me, I jumped in my newly purchased car and started my drive to Florida. As I approached Pelham, Georgia, driving in the left lane, I took my eyes off the road for a split second causing my car to drift toward the median at a speed of 65 mph. I attempted to regain control of the car, but I was forced into a tailspin –twice. I ended up back on the road at a dead stop facing oncoming traffic in the direction of Georgia with a car directly in front of me. What was I doing? Still facing in the direction of Georgia, and for an uncomfortable amount of time, I contemplated whether or not I should continue to Tallahassee. I battled with my decision. Was the universe speaking to me? I had to make a choice. I had a clear sign, yet ignorantly chose to continue to Tallahassee. .

After leaving Albany, Georgia, and being delayed, as a result of my road incident, I finally arrived on the campus of Florida State University (FSU).

Being an FSU undergraduate, I was all too familiar with the layout of the campus. At this point, I was drunk and wasn't thinking rationally. I drove my car over near the parking garage located across from the Seminole Soccer Complex. The complex is adjacent to the FSU Softball Complex which is located between Dick Howser Baseball Stadium and Mike Long Track. After exiting my car, I walked over to the parking garage, a place that I knew very well.

When I wanted to be alone, the garage was my place of refuge. It was also a place where I would sometimes go to work out and jog. Some days, I would go there to simply allow the cool breeze passing through the garage to hit my face and free my mind of all my negative thoughts. But today wasn't about any of that. I was on a mission to see Whitney, and I was going to do whatever it took to convince her to see me.

As I walked past the soccer field, I threw my keys onto the grass. By this time, there was no doubt that I was drunk. I was ready to say or do anything to persuade Whitney to see me. As foolish as it may sound, I was prepared to use suicide as a tactic of persuasion if necessary.

"In 2008, Whitney and I met for the first time in front of the FSU recreation center. I remember meeting her like it was yesterday. When we met in front of the FSU recreation center, I walked up to her and introduced myself. Something was drawing me to Whitney. The many light conversations we shared grew into us spending more time together. She mentioned to me early in our relationship that she contracted herpes as a result of being raped. This didn't stop me from wanting to be with her but a year into our relationship, I found out her rape story was a lie. I held that against her for a while and wondered what else she may have lied about and what the reason for the lie was. We dated off and on for about two years. I met her family and was eventually invited to a couple of family gatherings".

Desperate and not thinking clearly, I called her. She answered. I told her that I was in Tallahassee on the FSU campus. She responded by telling me she was at the pool party and had no plans of leaving to meet me. I told her that I was prepared to end my life by throwing myself off the parking garage roof if she didn't come.

None of this was about her. It was about me and my selfish desire to have the rape charges I was facing dropped (but little did I understand–dropping the charges was not her decision to make). Still on the phone, I told her that I loved her and continued to try and convince her to see me. After pleading with her, she finally decided to meet with me. Shortly after our phone conversation, she arrived at the FSU parking garage still wearing the bathing suit she wore to the pool party. We kissed and I told her that she looked great.

A few minutes later, I unclothed myself down to my boxers and told her that I was ready to go to the pool party with her. Clearly not in the right frame of mind, I walked over to the parking garage ledge and placed myself over the side doing pull-ups. Whitney did her best to remain calm suggesting that we get in the car. Although I wasn't thinking rationally, I wasn't prepared to commit suicide by throwing myself off the ledge. Ending my life was far from my objective. I eventually climbed back over the ledge to safety.

May 8, 2011, the rape victim contacted the lead investigator and informed him that the alleged suspect, Maurice Harris, was at an FSU garage on the top floor, threatening to jump. The investigator contacted the Florida State University Police Department and advised them of Harris' location. (Florida, 2021)

Whitney, being emotional and uncertain about what to do, walked up and embraced me. What I didn't know was that as we embraced with her phone to my back, she was sending a text message to the lead investigator involved in the rape allegation and giving him our location. Whitney had been instructed by the Tallahassee Police Department to call them if I made contact with her regardless of the circumstances.

2

GROWING UP IN THE HOOD

L looking back on my childhood, growing up in Homestead, a city located in South Florida nestled in the county of Miami-Dade, invites many memories. Homestead is represented by a crossroads of cultures; however, by no means is it the bustling metropolis that Miami is obviously known for. I came from a household with no father, three siblings, and with my mother, the matriarch.

At seventeen years old, my mom got married and started having children. She was still in high school when she became a wife, but was only married to my father for a few years. I'm not aware of the reason they divorced, but my father has had a reputation of being dishonest. He made a living with his construction and landscaping skills, yet, I've always questioned how his business survived. Dropping out of school in the eighth grade, his foundation as a business owner has always been unstable, to say the least.

Baby Maurice

When I was released from prison, I briefly worked with him although I was warned by several family members to be careful because of his dishonesty. I appreciated his offer to learn his skill; yet, quickly found out he wasn't knowledgeable about a lot of aspects of his own business. His business skills weren't the best and I wondered how he managed to operate some of the heavy machinery he used. He was supposed to be teaching me his trade, yet, through my observations, I knew he was doing whatever was necessary to get by with his limited expertise.

One thing I learned from my father is that a person can achieve a lot with nothing. Somehow, my father made it happen. He was able to make a living and run a business with minimum experience and a lot of manipulation. I knew I didn't want to follow in his footsteps as a businessman or a father. Unfortunately, my father figures have always been my football coaches from youth sports through college.

I had a lot of time to think while sitting in prison. I thought reestablishing my relationship with my father would bring some healing to both of us, so I attempted to reach out to him. I remembered his phone number which had not changed over the past twenty years. It felt good initiating the call, but the conversation never amounted to anything. He had plenty of excuses for not being a father to me as a child, but his excuses had run out. I was a grown man and he was still treating me like a child. Not only did his phone number not change, but he obviously had not changed either. I recall a few football games he came to and it almost felt like he was showing me off like I was his trophy football son. Was he proud of me, or was I simply making him look good? He sure didn't warrant any acknowledgment or credit for my athletic skills or accomplishments. He was from Miami but he moved around a lot; he never stayed in one place too long. He even did some jail time for a drug-related incident.

In the black community where social-economic inconsistencies are considered the norm, some would describe this as being the typical single-parent home.

13

Reflecting back on my adolescence and youth, my mom has always been my biggest supporter. Her support has never waned and remains ever-present in my life. By watching my mother and witnessing her determination to keep a roof over our heads, I'm certain my strong work ethic and desire to succeed came solely from her. I didn't come from a financially well-to-do family but my mother always made sure we had what we needed. Not a day went by when food wasn't on the table. Like many of the families in my neighborhood, we simply survived off what we had.

Today, it's a statistical fact that almost seventy percent of black children are born to single mothers. Those same mothers are far more likely than married mothers to be poor, even after a national post-welfare reform decline in child poverty. In the black community, that cycle far too often seems to repeat itself.

Being raised in the projects in South Florida or "the hood", my friends and I would sometimes find ourselves venturing out to places where we witnessed the ever-growing contrast between the have-and-have-nots. Stepping outside of my typical environment and seeing entire communities prospering really made me think about my own life and fulfilling all my hopes and dreams. After returning to the projects from my occasional journeys, I was quickly plunged back into reality surrounded by social-economic despair and hopelessness.

The art of survival in the projects forced me and many others to quickly learn how to navigate through both the good and bad. Seeing things at a young age such as young mothers with multiple children allowing men to come and go like revolving doors, and those same

14

mothers not understanding the impact of their children seeing such negative imagery is a cycle that continues to this day.

Unfortunately, seeing drug transactions was also a norm in my community. Drug use and alcohol abuse go hand-in-hand in the projects. As a young boy seeing people turn to drugs searching for their next fix or high, or watching an alcoholic hanging around at the corner store begging for change, felt like an inescapable reality. I must admit that having a group of close friends made it easy to navigate through my adverse surroundings. It allowed us to occasionally escape from what some might describe as dire straits and create occasional fun-filled moments.

I've been a physically active person for as long as I can remember and I haven't slowed down yet. Growing up, I was one of the most athletic and fastest runners in the neighborhood and everyone knew it. As a young boy, when I wasn't in school during the summer months,

I would wake up in the morning not really caring or paying much attention to the early morning family dynamics taking place around me. I guess you can say I was too busy being a kid. After breakfast, I would grab my football or something to play with and be quickly out the front door. I went to find my friends.

I remember walking many blocks in the South Florida heat and overflowing with excitement thinking about meeting up with friends to hang out, play, and burn off the endless amount of energy I had. We would play sports and just have fun doing "boy" things all day long. My friends were my family and no one could tell me otherwise. When we were together, it didn't matter what situations came up, right or wrong, we always looked out for one another. I was outgoing, adventurous, and like most boys, I was extremely curious about many things.

I've lost contact with most of my childhood friends, yet, I remember my first real friend, Sergio. Our mothers were close, so that brought us that much closer as friends. Because of our close family ties, Sergio's mother would also babysit me from time to time. We lived in the Sunset Projects which were located in a community called Naranja. Sergio and I went to the same school which was right across the street from the Projects.

After school, we spent most of our time together hanging out and looking for something to get into – the usual boy stuff. If you saw me, you saw Sergio. He was my partner and I recall many days where we played football together in the streets.

We would go from one community to another until we found a group of kids playing football in the streets. In the summers, we would wake early, go to a friend's house to play, or find somewhere interesting to go. If no one stopped us, we would play all day, tirelessly. We remained good friends from elementary school until we were in the fifth grade when his family moved to North Miami.

I hated to see him go. Sergio and I don't keep in contact anymore, but social media has allowed us to remain in contact with one another.

Another close friend I remember is Danny. We met at Campbell Middle School and as most people know or have experienced, middle school can be a challenging time for kids. Well, Danny and I handled those stressors of middle school together by skipping at least one class a day.

I had a very active and fun-filled childhood. Every day was like a new quest overflowing with excitement and endless exploration and sometimes leading me to places I had no business being. Most days, when I would leave the house in the morning and I wouldn't return home until it was almost dark or when the street lights came on…whichever came first. I truly enjoyed my time with my friends and it kept us out of trouble. Well…most of the time.

Living in the inner city, many parents used sports as a means of keeping their children physically active and away from potential trouble in the community. Many of the things I learned from sports involved self-discipline, teamwork, and other important life lessons. As a young kid, playing such sports as basketball and football was customarily something a lot of my friends and I loved doing.

As I continue to reflect back, many parents in my community involved their children in sports with the dream that they would one day leave Homestead and find themselves center stage and under the bright lights as the next great star athlete. Most of my friends and I played youth football together which was part of my initial introduction to team sports. Unlike a lot of my friends, I tried other sports such as wrestling and track and field.

In a short time, it became obvious to me and others that the game of football chose me and I responded; I showed no resistance. Because of my audacious nature, I didn't think there was anything I wasn't capable of doing. Because my mother worked so much, she wasn't able to attend most of my school and sporting activities. Leaving out the emotion, I simply accepted it for what it was.

17

On the other hand, my father and his untimely absence throughout my childhood and youth was something I learned to expect.

My Uncle Bobby was the one person who mentored and supported me throughout my adolescence and youth. He also provided that same support for many other kids in my community looking to achieve their goals of becoming productive citizens in society. The first time I remember meeting Uncle Bobby was in middle school. He came to recruit female student-athletes for his high school track team. I remember him always putting a great amount of emphasis on being a student-athlete. In other words, he made it clear that education was the main priority and not their athleticism.

In my freshman year in high school, Uncle Bobby wasn't the head football coach, but there was no doubt he was highly respected by both students and peers. However, he would eventually go on to become the head football coach. Looking back, I recall seeing hundreds of business cards he had from various universities and colleges. I'm not sure if he ever considered making the move to become a college football coach, but I'm certain that his main goal was to ensure all students had a chance to attend college and receive a quality education. He knew the only way to achieve academic excellence was through hard work and having above-average grades.

During his tenure as a head coach in 2005, at least ten of his student-athletes reached the NFL. Nearly ten times that same number have gone on to college and are now leading productive lives in various professions. This includes his son, Bobby McCray Jr., former free agent defensive end who played with the New Orleans Saints'

2009 Super Bowl championship team, and former Miami Hurricane Michael Barrow who played as a linebacker for twelve years in the NFL.

While playing high school football, I remember Uncle Bobby would bring in former NFL players he had relationships with as assistant coaches. This gave me a great advantage in the hope of one day achieving my ultimate goal of becoming an NFL star. Even when I moved up to Georgia, he continued to promote me to various colleges as a student-athlete. In reflection, it's apparent to me that Uncle Bobby was totally committed to giving back to his community by providing me and other students with an opportunity to see more of the world than just little Homestead, Florida.

Because my father's absence during most of my school events became a part of the norm, it caused me to be keenly aware of how not having him around impacted my life. My father was in and out of my life but never stayed around long enough to make a difference. I take full responsibility for my actions both good and bad, but I can't get the thought or idea out of my head about how not having my father around has mentally affected me.

There is no doubt that if a father figure was more prominent in my life and was there to teach me what disciple and accountability meant, maybe some of the challenges that I faced as a young man would have led to better decision-making. Instead, the development of my self- discipline and personal awareness came from my constant involvement with sports and building relationships with athletic coaches both on and off the field.

My mother never talked much about my father and I never asked about him. In my mind, I thought we were doing just fine without him. It wasn't until I grew older that I begin to think about my parents' relationship with one another and why my father failed at taking an active role in my life. In my mind, a father sets male structure – helps in the creation of formed discipline and the development of well- defined transitions of their sons from childhood to manhood.

As a boy, I was keenly aware that I was at risk for many things. I had many situations that arose where I felt the need for some form of male counseling and support that only a father could give. I eventually accepted the fact that my success or failure in life would be determined by me. During the time of the sexual assault,

I was 21 years of age, a college graduate, and an accused sex offender. It was during that time things began to unravel for me and it all occurred within a short period of seven months, shortly after receiving my bachelor's degree from Florida State University. To say I was sorry for my actions doesn't begin to describe just how remorseful I was. Yet, in my developing wisdom, I knew there was no adequate excuse, nor explanation…just circumstances.

Being in an explosive relationship and facing rape charges while ending a once-promising football future was primarily the result of an immature mind and not understanding my self-worth.

I allowed my lack of mental awareness, a depressive state of mind, and failure to control me. When I needed a reason to justify my illicit behavior by placing the blame on someone else, I did. My mother did her best to shelter me from harm, but there were certain things as a boy where I would have perhaps felt more comfortable or at ease sharing with my father. However, my character and the person I am today are a direct result of the many valuable lessons that I undoubtedly learned from my mother who started working at the age of fourteen.

It's reasonable to suggest that her upbringing played a role in the decision she made to start working at a fairly young age. Her decision was out of necessity. Seeing girls in my community working as young teenagers to support their families was a common occurrence in my community. Statistically speaking, it's something that occurs quite frequently in many of today's black low-income households. Growing up in a single-parent home in Homestead trying to make ends meet, my mother was forced to work two jobs. There were days and nights where I would only catch a glimpse of her. In fact, there were many days when my siblings and I wouldn't see her at all. It was a harsh reality that we all dealt with.

At the age of six, watching my mother struggle financially during those tough times, I began playing organized youth sports, specifically football. I recall overhearing my mother telling one of her friends, "One day, my baby is going to buy me a house." Her words ignited a real desire and determination in.

I started envisioning how one day my undeniable God-given athletic talents would be the catalyst in helping to propel my mother and our family out of poverty. Because my father was in and out of my life, I felt it was my responsibility to step up as a man and take care of my family.

Maurice, Kennithia (sitting) Dellaina (standing),
Mother and brother, Mark

3

TROUBLED DAYS

I remember looking through her phone and seeing messages suggesting she had sex with someone else days prior. Seeing those text messages angered me. I felt invalidated. The anger I was feeling caused me to commit an unspeakable act of sexual assault. This was the night that changed my life forever. After reading the text messages aloud to her, I recall feeling a sense of jealousy and rage. I wanted her to hear the words which caused me so much pain. I was hoping the words would make her feel sorry or regretful. I wanted her to hurt as much as I was hurting. The more I read, the more outraged I became. Text after text, I felt my anger intensify. I wasn't sure what she was feeling, but I felt a destructive storm approaching. In my mind, dark clouds were covering the sky, but the clouds were masking my ability to think rationally.

I was becoming someone I had never met. The sense of personal rejection I was feeling was overwhelming. How could she possibly do this to me? I felt as if I was having an out-of-body experience looking at someone I was totally unfamiliar with but at the same time looked similar to me. Emotionally, psychologically, and physically, I became the image of a person that had lost total control causing me to perform a heinous act – an act on a young woman I truly cared about. And that's when it happened.

> FSU PD officers located Harris and initiated the Baker Act. Harris had been found in just his boxer shorts, sitting on the top ledge of the parking garage on the third level. Harris had thrown all his clothes over the side and had told the victim he would jump if the police showed up. Shortly after threatening to take his own life, Harris was eventually talked down off the ledge by FSU Police Officers, apprehended by the Tallahassee Police Department, and transported to Memorial Hospital and within an hour, the Baker Act was rescinded by the examining doctor. Due to the pending investigation, the lead investigator was then contacted and informed regarding the rescinded Baker Act. *(Coley Harvey and Orlando Sentinel, 2011)*

Shortly after the sexual assault, it was as if a light bulb was turned on. Both Whitney and I began to realize the severity of the criminal charges I was facing. We both knew and understood the seriousness of the crime but felt it was purely an isolated incident and not representative of my true character. Because of that, Whitney and

I continued to be intimate with one another. Our relationship continued during my active house arrest while awaiting my trial date.

During the seven months that I was confined to house arrest, we attempted to salvage our relationship and began attending church together. Eventually, we came to the realization that our relationship was not sustainable and doomed for failure. That was pretty much the basis of our relationship. To say we were a toxic couple is an understatement – it was a tormentous bond. We both knew we needed to end our connection, but like a drug, we kept coming back for more. The relationship was initially a good thing, although, we both were mentally troubled to some degree. We masked our troubles with sex which allowed us to feel accepted by the other and avoid getting to know each other beyond small talk and sex. Having unorthodox sex was the norm for us.

"My mother didn't understand why I was still having sex with Whitney after the incident or why I was accepting visits from her after losing the trial. Whitney and I even talked about marriage two months into my prison sentence. My mother may not have understood but she kept a cordial relationship with Whitney".

The "good" in the relationship slowly dissipated and became explosive. The constant breaking up and getting back together became a pattern. It was the 'mentally troubled' part that kept bringing us back to each other knowing it was unhealthy. I had an immature mind and didn't want to fully walk away and start anew.

I guess the night she called the police was her way of waving the white flag. She had enough and I had done too much. Her decision for calling the police, in my mind, wasn't because she felt sexually violated or raped, but because she was ready to end the relationship.

Ending my relationship with Whitney was symptomatic of the criminal issues I would eventually have to face. With the law being the law, I knew my day of punishment was inevitable. Upon hearing all the facts during my pre-sentence hearing, the pre-sentence investigator (PSI) recommended no jail time resulting in my probation coupled with attending a mandatory anger management program.

Former Florida State LB Maurice Harris
Charged With Sexual Assault
By Coley Harvey and Orlando Sentinel

May 09, 2011

TALLAHASSEE - A former Florida State linebacker was arrested by Tallahassee police Monday, days after allegedly sexually assaulting a Tallahassee woman and threatening suicide.

Maurice Harris, 21, one-rising in FSU's linebacker corps, was charged with sexual battery following an arrest around midnight Monday morning. He is currently being held on $25, 000 bond.

The victim, a woman who is unnamed in an arrest and probable cause affidavit obtained by the Sentinel, alleges Harris forcibly raped her multiple times after she let him into her apartment Friday night.

The affidavit makes it clear the two had previous relationships, and that Harris may have been angered by the women's relations with another man.

The official report is closed pending investigation.

4

FINDING MYSELF

I was sixteen when my mother decided to uproot our family. We were leaving Homestead, Florida, and moving to Georgia. It all came as a shock to me because Florida was my home. That was where all my friends were. Before leaving Florida, I distinctly recall us doing things together as a family and thinking everything was fine. At the time, I had no idea about the many difficult challenges that my mother was faced with daily. I guess being the typical self-absorbed teenager and being too busy thinking about only myself, I didn't understand or comprehend the drastic change that was about to take place. My only question was...why?

Just reflecting back, it had to be the scariest time of my mother's life and mine as well. What would make my mother at 36 years of age, decide to uproot our family and move to Georgia without anything but hope and a drive?

Within six months of being in Georgia, I had attended two public schools and one alternative school. I was a teenager searching for my identity in life and moving to Georgia, away from my friends and usual surroundings, didn't help. Being placed in an alternative school with other teens that were there because of behavior issues did not result in its intended outcome. In fact, it had a profoundly negative impact on me. The major goal of an alternative school is to provide the students– not succeeding in the traditional classroom setting– a way to obtain academic credit, career exploration activities, vocational work experience, and extended teacher/peer support in an alternative setting where the ultimate goal is obtaining a high school diploma.

I decided that an alternative school wasn't for me. In my mind, it was primarily for bad kids and not a place I thought I should be. I ended up leaving my mother and two siblings and returning to Homestead, Florida - a place where I had grown up and, without question, was home to me. Upon my return to Homestead, I moved in with a friend and teammate I had previously lived with. I lived there briefly until my Uncle Bobby who was the head football coach at the high school I was attending allowed me to stay with him.

Unfortunately, this didn't last long. The idea of having to abide by someone's house rules didn't sit too well with me. I ran the streets a lot and quite often wouldn't come home until the following day. Another concern my uncle had was, I didn't get along with his assistant coaches. Because of that, I was oftentimes not coachable. Quite frankly, I wasn't in the right frame of mind which resulted in me choosing to temporarily suspend all my sports involvement including football, and opting to live on the streets. I had friends and other family members that would have allowed me to live with them, but choosing not to was purely my decision.

During the many personal struggles I was dealing with, I was not going to allow anything or anyone to stand between me and getting my high school diploma. It just wasn't going to happen! Being on the streets of Homestead for about a week, I did what I could to support myself. Throughout those turbulent times, I somehow managed to make it to my senior year of high school. While on the streets, to pay all my graduation senior expenses I sold marijuana and gambled. Eventually, I smoked up all the marijuana I intended to sell.

One day while still on the streets, I decided to walk about three miles to my friend's house to rest. As I approached his house and knocked on the door, he opened it and immediately began to visually scan me up and down. He stated to me that I looked like crap. Because he was clearly aware of my situation, without hesitation, he told me I could stay with him, so I did. Because of our friendship and close family ties, I felt completely at home. In the second semester of my senior year in high school, I left my friend's house and moved in with my father.

I had mixed emotions about moving in with him, but I was willing to set my emotions aside with hopes of renewing our relationship. I was under no grand illusion that my father was going to somehow turn into the man I wished he had been in the past.

After moving in with him, we rarely saw one another. I realized that nothing would ever change the memories of growing up without a father's love, support, and influence, and even if we did attempt to forge a relationship, I still couldn't undo his absence during my childhood. Besides, during those difficult times, I had my girlfriend and my gifted athletic abilities which made me more focused and excited about my possible future endeavors academically, and I was one of the top high school football prospects in the state of Florida.

My overwhelming love for sports, particularly football, became very apparent at a young age. My mother helped to foster a love for sports and supported me every step of the way. She involved me in various sporting activities as a child, including taking me to many sporting events and supplying me with whatever I needed to advance my interest. My mother never wavered in her belief that education was the number one priority for all her children and everything else came second.

Maurice's mother

Cynthia Harris

South Miami in the 1990s was known as a hotbed filled with top high school football prospects and I was one of them. My highlight years were when I began to be recognized as a standout athlete beginning in 1996. I was known in my community for being a great athlete. I was always ready to challenge anyone who thought they were better than I was. People in the neighborhood would gather, both young and old, to watch me show off my athlete talents. I was destined for greatness and knew it.

During the years between 1996 and 2003, I lived in four different homes and attended five high schools. It was also the time when I started to run the streets with my friends and occasionally get into mischief. Being the product of a single-parent home and not having my father around wasn't helpful either in terms of the self-discipline that I was lacking.

I played football for the newly established Naranja Ravens youth football team in the Orange Bowl Football League. After summer football ended and the new school year began, my friend Danny and I started spending more time outside of the classroom. We hung out in the school hallways, off-campus during school hours, and ran the streets of Leisure City. We would leave the school grounds and eventually return to campus before the school day ended. It was during these times that I started to struggle in school academically. We had fun skipping school, but we later paid for it. Danny eventually got kicked out and sent to an alternative school, and I was held back and had to repeat the seventh grade.

One of the main pivotal points in my life came when I was held back as a seventh-grader. I knew I was failing and that I would probably have to repeat the seventh grade before being told. My mother even told me, "Repeat the seventh grade, repeat the same clothes." Knowing how brutal students can be watching their peers fail academically and making fun of them was something I didn't want to face. I also didn't like the idea of physically being the biggest kid in class either. Immediately, I thought of ways to expedite my placement into the eighth grade before the school year ended.

For some reason, I was chosen to be the school counselor's aide. To this day, I don't know why they chose me. I took advantage of the opportunity and pleaded with the counselor daily to put me in the correct grade. She encouraged me to get my grades up and maintain them and promised I would be in my correct grade the following semester.

After working really hard, meeting with teachers and taking the counselor's advice, I was allowed to complete an extra semester in the seventh grade and was placed in my correct grade the following semester just as the counselor promised. I never had a problem getting my homework done or excelling in school, but getting my school work wasn't my focus – having fun was my focus. At first, I didn't take school very seriously and didn't apply myself as well as I should have. It wasn't until I reached high school that I realized the significance of having a good education.

In large part, it was my sheer determination and persistence that eventually led to me being placed back into the eighth grade. I felt the need to redeem myself during summer school but failed in doing so because of an incident involving an alleged sexual assault. The result of which led to being terminated from the summer school program.

Knowing how good of an athlete I was, my coaches' willingness to use money as a means of persuasion and convincing my mother that too much idle time, wasn't good for me–in time, they were able to persuade my mother to allow me to play. Because of being kicked out of the summer school program, my mom "terminated" me from playing sports as a consequence for my actions. My mom was a stickler for us doing well in and staying in school.

After my promotion to the eighth grade I decided to join the wrestling team. The wrestling team was coached by men that took the sport very seriously. They believed that nothing was more important than having a winning attitude.

Wrestling provided me with the opportunity to learn something new, and at the time, helped to keep me physically conditioned during the football offseason. I fought to secure a spot in the 155-pound weight class and become a member of the wrestling team. And I did just that. My team and I lost the first overall team competition, so the coaches and the team quickly became more focused during practice at South Dade High School. The coaches also made sure that the team knew academics came before athletics.

From that point going forward, we won every team competition that year and won both District and County team competitions in Miami Dade.

The speech given by the head coach after winning both events was one to remember. There was one sentence in it where the head coach stated, "It's sad to say, after this weekend some of you may be arrested, because of the free time and built up energy. Find something productive to do, channel that energy, and stay out of trouble". Two days later, I was arrested and charged with several felony offenses stemming from a school incident involving a fight that I was not initially a part of.

The fight occurred on Monday, March 17, 2003. I and other onlookers were there when the fight initially began. I didn't know either of the two students involved in the fight. For no apparent reason, I decided to kick one of the students lying on the ground. Before I realized it, I was quickly snatched and removed from the crowd by a police officer assigned to the school. I was only thirteen at the time and weighed approximately 155 pounds. I was tossed around by the police officer and slammed to the ground several times. I was eventually thrown into a car and told to stop resisting. After what seemed like an eternity of being aggressively handled by the officer, I calmed down after several of the students pleaded with me to stop resisting. I was placed in handcuffs, taken into custody, and driven away.

After arriving at the police station, I was quickly booked and charged with battery on an officer, battery, disorderly conduct, and resisting arrest with violence. I was processed and locked up for a couple of days before getting picked up by my mother.

Unfortunately, this was one of many future felony offenses I would find myself involved in.

My freshman year, I wanted to walk onto the junior varsity football field and attempt to be a receiver because of my speed. Although I played linebacker growing up, no one at the high school level knew me because I came from a different community. It became quite obvious after watching me drop three passes during practice that my career as a receiver was not going to happen. Because of my wrestling skills, I was told that maybe I would do well on the defensive side of the ball. Playing defensive linebacker, I began to flourish. After two games of junior varsity, I was moved to varsity as second string middle linebacker. Being moved to varsity also allowed me to play with my brother who was the starting defensive end. The next year, my sophomore year, I was moved to safety. This same year, my brother became starting middle linebacker; we shared exceptional athleticism.

After my sophomore year, my mother decided to move to Georgia. Since I was from South Florida, a place known for producing great athletes, I was placed on the field with great expectations from the coaches and players. My first three games were good and I didn't disappoint but I got injured. It seemed as if everyone turned their backs on me because I could no longer perform as expected. I felt like I had no support and no friends. I wondered if I was liked only because of my athletic skills. I wasn't in a good place mentally and slipped into depression. My sadness was acted out in the form of bad behavior (flipped over a table and went home) and I got suspended. I ended up in an alternative school where a football program was non-existent.

At the end of my junior year and with my mother's permission, I moved back to Homestead. My senior year in high school playing football was terrific. I was the captain on defense, and I had the trust of both players and coaches. I played on both sides of the ball, but in most games, I rarely left the field. Looking back, there were times when I burnt out. At that point, I had given the game of football all that I had, and then some. My mother, living in Georgia, would drive down to Homestead to watch me when she could. There were days when I felt lonely not having her around. Occasionally, my dad would come around and fill a small void.

I also excelled at wrestling. I loved wrestling more because it was an individual matchup, you against another opponent. New to the sport of wrestling, I did well until I got hurt. I was ranked nationally as a standout football player and got the attention of various collegiate schools. I was scouted and recruited by some of the nation's top Division I collegiate programs including Wisconsin, Arizona State, Rutgers, Ole Miss, and Florida State. I visited with a few of the schools recruiting me. My first two visits were to Wisconsin and Arizona State. My visit to both places was more about partying than football recruitment.

During my visits to Florida State, Rutgers, and Ole Miss, I mainly stayed in the dorm and just relaxed. I had partied enough during my previous visits. Florida State was my last visit and I chose to sign with them primarily because it placed me close to my mother's home in Albany, Georgia.

Maurice Harris, 6-0, 220, LB, Homestead Rivals Top 100 in the state of
Florida and a three-star prospect...Scout.com has Harris rated the 24th-best
prospect at his position in 2007...Rivals list him as one of the top 40 outside
linebackers in the nation in 2007...ran the 40 in 4.4, benches 300 pounds and has a
35" vertical leap...won the Spark competition at the NIKE combine in Miami
finishing first among 400 athletes...had 112 tackles, 12 sacks, four forced fumbles,
and one (1) interception in 2006...named first-team All-Dade, first-team all-state,
Defensive MVP, Homestead News Leader's All-Star Team and was selected to
play in the All-American Bowl and Dade/Broward All-star classic...also wrestled
in high school winning the Dade County wrestling tournament...chose FSU
over North Carolina, Ole Miss, Arizona State, Rutgers, NC State, Pittsburgh, and
Wisconsin (247sports.com).

Before receiving all the recruitment letters, I was just playing football because I was good at it. In 1996, my first year of playing organized football, I can still recall my mother telling me that I was going to buy her a home. At the time, I didn't have a real plan to take care of my mother, but I was convinced that football was going to be the catalyst I used.

A few months before my graduation from high school, my girlfriend got pregnant. Because we were young and totally unprepared for parenthood, we decided together to have an abortion. Being older and knowing what I know now, I understand abortion was not the only solution. We continued to see one another during my freshman year in college, but we both realized that the distance between us was too much to overcome, so we decided to end our relationship and remain friends.

On February 7, 2007, I committed and signed a letter of intent to Florida State University.

Doak Campbell Stadium
photo credit:
www.nolefan.org

During that same year former Seminole Todd Stroud, who played nose guard for FSU (1983-85) was appointed to the Strength and Conditioning program at FSU. Coach Stroud was considered one of the top strength and conditioning coaches in the nation and I would have the opportunity to train under him. My set-up for success in football couldn't get any better.

Coach Stroud was named the 2000 National Strength and Conditioning Association's Conference USA Professional of the Year. He was also a nominee for the National Strength and Conditioning Professional of the Year Award. As an athlete, to be mentored and trained by the best was a dream come true for any young man wanting to further their football career. I was there! My chance to make my NFL dream a reality was in my hands. I knew I would have access to knowledge and skill training that countless young men only dream of. For me, this was unquestionably a dream come true.

Coach Todd Stroud (Photo) Nolefan.org

Regretfully, my immaturity, lack of personal awareness, and unwise choices led to a series of unfortunate events, turning all of my earned opportunities into a personal nightmare. Regrets? Of course, I have regrets, who wouldn't?

I try my best not to think about the life I could have had, but the daily reminders are undoubtedly there. The challenges I faced restoring the semblance of my prior life, helped me to rediscover my true character and reminded me that I'm not the person many people see me as. Nevertheless, my unfortunate choices caused me to fumble my only chance. My poor decision-making not only deterred my dreams but changed my life in ways I never imagined.

In 2019, Coach Stroud was the assistant head coach and defensive line coach for the Miami Hurricanes. During that time, we stayed in touch. Watching him at Miami reminded me of his impact on me at Florida State. He is the true definition of what it means to be a coach and more importantly, a mentor. He understood training and coaching is not solely on the football field, but how each player had a life off the field, and displayed character traits that solemnly shadowed them during practices and games.

Former Florida State LB Maurice Harris Charged
With Sexual Assault

Florida State backup linebacker Maurice Harris was arrested Monday night and charged with two felonies and one misdemeanor, according to Major Jim Russell of the Florida State University Police Department.

Harris, who was charged with grand theft, possessing a vehicle with altered numbers and a non-moving traffic violation has been suspended indefinitely, the University announced Tuesday.

"We're suspending Maurice Harris, indefinitely, beginning today until the matter has been resolved," Coach Bobby Bowden said in a statement. The University said it would have no further comment.

On June 17, University parking services put an immobilization device – basically a parking boot – on a motorcycle on the FSU campus. The boots are used when drivers have outstanding parking fees or lingering fines that have to be paid. On June 18, parking services noticed the motorcycle and the boot were gone, according to police.

"Those things are $300 or more apiece," Russell said. "If someone takes them off, that's considered to be a theft."

On Monday, parking services noticed the motorcycle parked near Gate A at the stadium and notified the police at 4:34 p.m. An officer contacted strength and conditioning Coach Todd Stroud, who had borrowed the motorcycle from Harris earlier in the day. Stroud brought Harris in to talk to the officer, but Harris refused to talk to him and denied knowing anything about the boot, according to police.

45

The vehicle identification number had also been scratched off, so Harris was charged with possession of a vehicle with altered numbers. The paper tag on the bike was also not assigned to it, so that was a misdemeanor charge. The theft of the boot and the other charge were both felonies. The motorcycle has been impounded, but police still aren't sure to whom it belongs.

"Without any other information, we don't know who it belongs to at this point," Russell said. "We haven't gotten to the bottom of that."

In addition to his arrest charges, Harris, a redshirt sophomore, had only played in six career games, and he's been hindered by injuries. He played in three games in 2007 but injured his knee, and a nagging ankle injury limited him to three games the previous year.

Upon Harris' return to the team during the fall of 2009, after being arrested June of that same year, his football playing days officially ended at FSU after a neck injury against Georgia Tech forced the Seminoles to deem him medically disqualified (*Orlando Sentinel, 2011*).

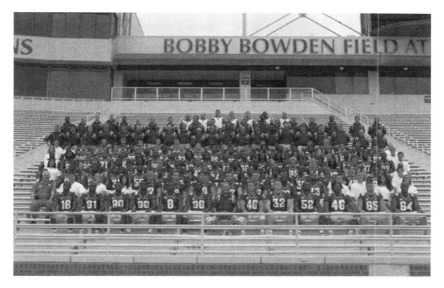

2007 Florida State Football Team

(Nolefan.org)

Coach Bobby Bowden,
the winningest football
coach in Florida State History.

Academically, my year in college went well. Grades to ratio, I was considered one of the smart ones on the football team. My grades in college were never a concern. We went by a sliding scale to qualify for college and my GPA was a 3.0, SAT 890, and an ACT of 21.

After seeing other football players who were recruited as defensive linebackers like myself, I immediately began to realize that I was physically undersized for a typical Division I linebacker.

Because I was the typical promo – type, I relied on my athleticism and strong work ethic to push me forward. In high school, I was always one of the top ten aggressors on every team I played on, but it didn't translate well to the Division I collegiate level and I knew it.

Although I was considered to be undersized for my position, I knew I had to showcase myself by letting my athleticism shine on the field, and I did just that. In 2009, I became one of the key contributors on the field at FSU. That spring, I was the Iron Nole winner on defense and was battling for a starting job as a sophomore.

Maurice was often hurt during his career at FSU, earning a medical redshirt and suffering through nagging ankle injuries as, a redshirt freshmen.

"I knew that I was small for the linebacker position I played at FSU. I relied on my athleticism and strong work ethic to push me forward."

Maurice Harris

Off the field, I was viewed by many as a model student-athlete. I was one of FSU's most active members of athlete community service initiatives, even receiving the ACC Top Six for Service Award. In Tallahassee, I volunteered with programs like Special Olympics, Upward Bound, and Capital City Youth Services. I received those awards, yet not long afterward, I was standing before a judge about to be awarded sentencing for a sexual assault crime.

Maurice "Smiley" Harris, supporting and entertaining
FSU's community youth

Maurice volunteered with programs like Special Olympics, Upward
Bound, and Capital City Youth Services.

Maurice, his mom, and siblings

5

THE TRIAL

Although Whitney admitted she "allowed" the sex, I was charged with sexual battery. She appeared in court, not as my ex-girlfriend but as the victim. My mother was also in court with me. Being in court was surreal. I felt like I was watching a movie. This type of thing happened to other people, not me. I'd been in court before, but never before a criminal judge. This time was different, much different. I was supposed to be on the football field – behind the line of scrimmage. I was supposed to be on the football field defending the goal, yet, I was in court attempting to defend my character and protect my future. I had a public defender only after the one lawyer Whitney found for me said I didn't have a case.

During a break, after all of the evidence was presented, I took my mom, Whitney, and her sister out to eat. We ate at Olive Garden. I told Whitney that I lost the case and she said she wished she was pregnant. As much as I appreciated her sentiments, whether true or not, my focus was somewhere else – on my future which was in the hands of twelve strangers – the jury. I knew in my heart and mind that I would be found guilty.

The prosecutor said he felt it was important to pursue the rape charges despite the victim's reluctance to testify. The case is "state versus Maurice Harris" not the woman versus Maurice Harris, he said. Harris is scheduled to be sentenced December 6th.

In less than 30 minutes which seemed like forever, the jury completed their deliberation and reached a verdict. I anxiously stood to hear the verdict. I quickly glanced at the faces of the twelve people who determined my next steps in life and just as I thought, I was found guilty. The word "guilty" echoed in my mind repeatedly as I faced the judge. My belt was then removed and I was handcuffed before I left the courtroom. I handed my belt to my mother who was with Whitney and they were both crying.

I could only imagine what was going through my mother's mind when I handed her my belt and she watched me walk away. This time, the circumstances were quite different. I didn't look back because there was nothing she could do; she could not rescue me. Without delay, I was transported to the county jail to await sentencing - a month later.

6

LOOKING BACK

I think back on my college days often with regret, but sometimes I choose not to beat myself up and relish the fact that I was recruited to play for a Division I college. Not just any college, but Florida State. I don't watch football at all now and it was never a sport I had a deep passion for, but it was a means to an end. It was my avenue to make a better life for myself and my family. The sequence of events that happened in my life molded me into the man I am today. The people I crossed paths with, the coaches who poured into me, and those who supported me when I was at my lowest are all key factors in my progression in life.

The rape incident is definitely a key factor. I consider my sexual experiences as a young child and wonder if any of those young foolish days played a part in my actions – the actions that caused me to carry the title and weight of a sex offender for the rest of my life. I recall my first sexual encounter which was while I was in middle school. I was thirteen years old and my high school days were quickly approaching. I didn't mind going to high school, but what I did mind was going to high school as a virgin – that couldn't happen.

At thirteen, I didn't know anything about sex, but I had a cousin who was about five years older than I was and our conversations planted the idea of sex in my mind. I had a girlfriend at the time, but instead of asking her, I had friends who told me about a girl who had a reputation for having sex. She was twelve years old, which was only a year younger than I was but she was still in elementary school. I didn't fully understand it then but I knew something wasn't right with her still being in elementary school. I boldly asked her if she would have sex with me and she agreed with no questions asked. I rode my bike to her house and surprisingly found all my friends there. I wasn't afraid of having sex for the first time, but once I arrived at her house, seeing my friends there was unnerving.

Her reputation obviously had truth to it. I asked her to go into another room with me away from everyone else. Looking at her, I must have felt sorry for her, or maybe it was guilt, but I asked her why she had sex with everyone. Her reply was that she liked it. Her answer told my 13-year-old mind that it was okay to be like the other boys and use her body. It was as if her answer validated my actions. I pulled out the condom I had in my pocket and took advantage of the opportunity the young girl offered.

I don't remember where I got the condom from, but I was going to ensure I wasn't going to high school a virgin.

It wasn't an enjoyable first experience to remember because the only thing I really remember is how my friends kept busting in the room like it was a game or something. Thinking back, there were no adults around that house – absolutely no supervision at all. We were minors having sex with minors. Shouldn't an adult be held accountable? Surely, minors aren't in a position to make adult decisions. Where was the crime there and who is held responsible?

As hard as I've tried to remove another childhood incident from my mind, that unsupervised home triggers taunting thoughts in my head of a disturbing incident I briefly mentioned in my journal. Besides my mother, only two other people are aware of this painful memory I carry. One of those people is Whitney. After the rape incident, she found a need to share my secret pain with my mother.

The triggered memory is that of me being molested by an older cousin. I don't remember my specific age, but I was around eleven or twelve years old. I've tried my best to completely erase the memory from my brain, but I can recall it vividly. My babysitter's son talked me into following him in the bathroom. He closed the door and convinced me to give him oral sex. Unbeknownst to me why, I agreed. I don't remember how often it happened, but I remember a confused young boy following the leader with no questions asked.

The reason Whitney felt a need to share this with my mother is because she thought the molestation may have been a contributing factor associated with why I raped her. She may be correct, but it doesn't remove the fact that I was found guilty of the crime.

When my mother found out, she blamed herself. No matter how many times I told her I owned my actions, she still felt responsible as most mothers probably would. As a single mother, she couldn't watch me and my siblings all the time. Her priority was taking care of us, which required working around the clock to make sure there was food on the table for us to eat and a roof over our heads for shelter.

I never publicly mentioned the molestation until now. Writing about it in prison was my way of self-therapy. Now, I know that journaling was my way of relieving psychological tension I wasn't aware I had. Journaling was therapeutic for me and as difficult as it was, it led to a lot of personal growth.

I know, through my own reading and research, that child molestation can leave long-term effects on the victim. I can honestly say, I've experienced several of the researched effects but didn't realize it was due to being molested Being a victim who attempted to suppress and ignore the molestation act itself, I now accept it's not something that will be easily erased from my mind. Being molested as a child will have some type of impact on me for the rest of my life. I also believe some of the listed effects may be from the time I spent in prison.

Back when I was sixteen in Albany, Georgia lacking the notoriety I had in South Florida (Homestead), I attempted to engrave the letter S on my chest. I said it stood for Smiley, Super, Supreme, Saved, or something like that. The process of my homemade tattoo took too long and hurt too bad for me to make a lasting mark. I soon realized it wasn't the letter S I wanted, but it was a form of self-inflicted pain that felt soothing to me.

The attempted tattoo wasn't an isolated incident. Sure, I may have wanted the tattoo, but deep inside I wanted relief. It was a form of dealing with internal pain. I'm not sure if I was feeling angry, anxious, or frustrated because I wasn't getting the attention I had in South Florida on the football field. As dangerous and unhealthy as it was, I did it. It was also soothing as I released built- up tension while punching walls, hitting, or cutting myself.

My wounds were unspoken words. Maybe even cries for help. I punched a wall many times when I felt like I opened myself up too much in a relationship and was denied in any way. Throughout my life I have intentionally hurt myself, sometimes to get temporary attention from individuals, but mostly to prove something to myself. I will not forget the things that I have gone through and I remember them because I wear them almost literally on my sleeves.

7

JOURNALING BEHIND BARS

Regardless of what anyone else said or thought, I felt like I owed Coach Stroud an apology. Unfortunately, the apology letter was never mailed and he never received the letter. Surprisingly, writing the letter did serve its purpose – it made me acknowledge and reflect on the opportunity I missed. I had time for a lot of reflection over my life because the letter was written while serving time for a crime which changed the course of my life. The aforementioned choices, which I completely own, led me to serve a prison sentence.

My years of incarceration taught me lessons I practice to this day. Many of the lessons I learned during my incarceration involved humility and the value of personal freedom. However, the single most important lesson I learned during my incarceration was understanding how vulnerable and unprepared I was for relating to unforeseen problematic life events. Many of those events and challenges had the capability of changing my life's journey and trajectory and led me down a path causing me to question my life and my purpose in it.

Others were instrumental in setting me up for success. I thought of them often as I sat behind the prison walls and still do. Will an apology change anything? Probably not, but it allows for peace in my spirit knowing I at least acknowledged those who made an effort to either guide, direct, mentor or coach me. I was on a path to be great, to achieve unrealized goals, and play in the NFL. From little league football to the Florida State Seminoles.

I look back at my life and realize what major impact sports had on it. Sports kept me occupied, but unfortunately not enough to keep me out of trouble. I found myself standing before a judge numerous times as a young boy. From fighting in middle school to trespassing on private property, I was far from being a menace to society; however, the roots of those mischievous acts came back to haunt me later in life.

As I aged, I thought the active energy would settle a bit, but it didn't. The seeming overabundance of chemical and kinetic energy flowing through my body only changed form as I grew older; it seemed to intensify. Many athletes will admit that without a rigorous regime of exercise or some form of vigorous activity, energy is built up anticipating an outlet for release. If there is no available source for discharge, an outlet will be created and hopefully, it's a positive one. The steam must blow, which is why many athletes drink and smoke excessively - to occupy that never-ending flow of energy. Sports kept me grounded.

My entire football career (ages 6- 20) was an accumulation of bad hits, minor injuries, and stingers. The hits finally took their toil in college. Entering a game where my position had to hit the opposition every single play became a hard task once my entire left side of my body went numb. I was snatched from the game thinking it was a break when in reality it was the last football game I would ever again suit up for. Just seeing my teammates get ready and suit up was heartbreaking. I had a constant reminder of my injury when I put my chin to my chest, which created a tingling sensation throughout the entire right side of my body.

It was difficult working out, and it seemed as though no one really cared. I created a shell that included smoking weed, drinking, and having sex. My college degree was chosen by football, the university was because of football, my body was football. Who could understand the rise and fall of a mere college athlete? Sidelined, with no one around that could relate to my circumstances, I decided to end the game of football.

The memory of not having feelings in my legs and potentially becoming paralyzed because of football was more than enough to

validate my decision to walk away from my dream of one day

playing in the NFL. I was never fully content with my decision and always felt as if I was a quitter. I spiraled into bad habits which resulted in eight years in prison. Was there any good to be found in it? The eight years invited an intimate time of introspection through journaling.

Cameron Meller Photography

Day one of prison sentence began with me and other inmates being driven over to what's known as the prison reception area at Blackwater River Correctional facility often referred to as Camp Cupcake. Blackwater River Correctional Facility is a private state prison in Santa Rosa County, Florida, which opened in 2010. The facility houses about 2000 inmates. It was during that time the realization of my conviction as a sex offender began to take hold of me. The idea of me going from being a Division I football student-athlete at Florida State University and becoming a convicted sex offender was something that I couldn't begin to imagine happening. During my initial processing, I could see the blatant fear and uncertainty in the eyes of many of the new prisoners. Those types of emotions were far from my mind.

I remember thinking to myself, I'm really here and how do I find my way out legally. I knew I was facing difficult times and deservedly so, thus began my sentence and journey to personal redemption.

pic credit: northescambia.com (online news)

DOCUMENTING MY DAYS

Below are unedited and personal documented pages from my personal journal that I kept while in prison. (For the purpose of publishing, punctuation and missing words may have been added to be more readable.) It may sound like I'm rambling and some may make no sense at all, but my late night and early morning notes were my personal thoughts and never meant to be publicly shared. Journaling was a way to clear my mind and keep my peace of mind while imprisoned.

It is now approximately seven o clock in the morning C.S.T–the last day of the year 2016. Tomorrow, I would be able to think and state that I will be released from prison next year, after a little over 5 years of being locked up. I have not eaten in nearly 60 hours and drank my first drop of water about six hours ago. My last 76 hours of 2016, I wished to detoxify my body, mind, and spirit. No eating or drinking for 48 hours, then flushing out with water the last 24 hours.

One may ask why, to those that understand sacrifice can comprehend my abstaining from the body's basic needs, nourishment that can cloud the mind and veil the spirit. To reiterate that I can do without gave me the courage to go on with more caution and less fear. This courage will allow me to swallow my fanciful pride, giving without restraint, to those less fortunate, though my time is comparatively short; it can be extended with one simple false move. Removing, temporarily, a necessity, helps gradually remove unnecessary wants.

I have many goals for the New Year. I would like to improve my physical flexibility, allowing me to control my body in more meaningful movements. I also will like to finish writing a book, I began formulating in 2012. Of those I have talked to and heard their stories, these men have inspired me, giving me hope and strength to push through the irrelevant to capture what truly matters. The last five years have brought clarity to my dull vision. I have moved from the edge of the darkness and absorbed some light. I know now the light takes time to fully understand, it is we that choose darkness, the radiance is always there for our comfort. Patience and positivity have brought me peace, now I may move forward in confidence.

1/2/17

I can finally say that I going home next year, to spend time with my true love ones. I'm now able now to distinguish between love and lust. Lust, I allowed to occupy my time and energy, which lead me to prison. Love is that which energizes and never tires.

1/3/17

Just heard another inmate died with only 5 months left on his sentence. A reminder that time is not promised, this one did drugs; yet, the other from a couple of weeks back collapsed while playing basketball, had complained of heart pains.

Yet, it took twenty minutes for him to be removed from the Recreation yard, minutes later he died of a heart attack. Must pay attention to others, my insides, and myself, and outside can show signs of danger.

1/13/17

Last night, I spoke to my brother and was very disappointed at his reaction to adversity.

To broaden your horizon - expands mental perceptions or possibilities and example is to look at negative things as opportunities to receive a positive result.

1/16/17

I'm thinking entirely too much, though maybe not enough. I am beginning to get anxious about going home, with a whole lot of time to do in prison, the what ifs are starting to accumulate. My mind is creating solutions without factual basis. I'm hoping things will happen without knowing what has happened in the last five years.

The world has changed without me being a part of it. I have been forgotten and remembered by those I cannot even guess. I must keep up my guard for trivial prison occurrences, though, confidentiality seems obsolete.

1/21/17

I was torn between writing the coming words or not before, though, now I say, "why not".

Early December, I begin receiving letters from a pastor stating that he opened a home for men having trouble finding a place to stay because of their sex offender status. This had been a relief because I have heard others stating it will be difficult. This pastor's words were a breath of fresh air. I shared his message, even imagined getting knowledge and experience to open my own home for men struggling to find a home right out of prison. The pastor asked me to tell him about myself, I thought to gauge my attitude and demeanor, so I opened up expressing my future goals and my dream to become very successful by publicizing things others usually try to keep secret. Unfortunately, this pastor took my opening up as an open door to a possible relationship. He became very explicit and shared some uncomfortable things about his intentions and his plans for he and me. I wrote back expressing my apologies and true intention... He did not write me back.

1/26/17

An obvious trait to see by an observer is when an inmate tries to drown his misery of being in prison. I may have touched on this subject before though two antidotes brought to my attention was, one eating and two, working.

As I thought about those two vehicles, I also thought of a possible one that I should consider and be aware of, seeing other's faults. We may do things obsessively to hide the true pain we try to hide. We must come to terms with our current situation, learn from it be reminded of it though–move on to a better path

2/1/17

I believe I cannot limit this to only inmates, though I realize it more and more as I talk to others it can be seen as multiple things psyching ourselves out, either faith or whatever.I'm here for a reason If I did not come here, I would be dead, this saved my life. This time here is priceless

Most of us say these things to feel better about our current situation. We must say these things to accept a reality we really do not want to be in. Because more than not if we can choose to be released at this point, we will. This type of thinking, I came to hear then realized, is what drives people towards their goals–the constant belief that something is going to happen in the future to make all the good deeds and hard work worth it.

2/2/17

I have just received my final court document, and was surprised to feel the thickness of it because I was expecting another rubber stamp, as all other courts have done. While reading I saw that the courts are more thorough than

I believe any inmate give them credit for, as I read I saw, in my mind's eye every imaginary crack close, all the illusionary loop holes become a straight seal line. I also read about and saw the person people will see when they look at me. I will now be judged by the words written describing a scene only a psycho would display.

2/3/17

I am on my sixty third month and even now I am delusional; the above entry is only a half-truth: I did the crime I was charged with period. I did it, and until this moment, I did not want to accept it. I said it plenty of times, though I never accepted that full truth. I still feel the need to fight, fight for what? I don't know, I know and believe that I have to move on, stop hiding behind the fact that I was bonded out by the victim, that we had sex afterwards, that she said she wanted to be a victim that she didn't fight me off as much as I think she should have. Whitney smith middle name Lashaye was a victim at that time and I was her rapist. So now, I will be a sex offender for the rest of my life. I shall live with the consequences of my actions. It is sad that it took me 63 months—approximately one thousand eight hundred and ninety days—to write the truth down on paper, so that it will not be just a fleeing thought. I am not in the best situation, but I am definitely not in the worst.

As of right now, this moment is bittersweet; however, I know the 5 years of bitterness will be gone in only a fraction of that time because my engrained goals are positivity and happiness in all and every situation or circumstance. I must compare my situation with the famous Magic Johnson: he was living a life, which lead to a mistake that he is reminded of everyday. Yet what does he do, he accepted it, learned to live with it then helped others while benefiting from it himself. If he did it, why do I doubt myself, I can do it as well; I will do it as well. This is that which I will hope for without being able to see. I am a sex offender. I have done the crime, I will do the time, I will help others to not make my mistakes and if they have, help them move forward from them at the same time benefit from it. I will KEEP HOPE ALIVE!

2/3/17

It begin as a game of lessons, then become an obsession with me: observing living others faults then finding ways to learn from them Now that it has become to feel like a barrier between others and me, I remember burying my dirt under others. I have attempted and accomplished running away from my own problems. My coping mechanism was to exploit other persons coping devices. Make sure I see and express what was wrong with them so that I would not see what was wrong with my thinking.

2/5/17

Yesterday, I finally felt the urge to let go, so I begin a purging of things I have been holding on to for more than five years. Between yesterday and today, I have quartered about three thousand pages of my legal documents and letters. Every time I opened my lockers and glanced at the folders, I would hope my saving the papers would be worth it. However, now I have been forced to realize, that I should begin to create new memories. The said documents have been helping that helped me do more than half of my sentence. Why, should I ask for more? I was ignorantly asking for the truth to be hidden so that I may happily live a lie. Each and overtime I added to my main folder, hopefully beneficial true worthwhile endeavors.

2/10/17

We have been forced to be optimistic as inmates knowing that to be put in a situation thinking it is, as punishment will only make the

situation punish us constantly. Though to state, believe then show that all situations can be positive is setting us up for successes and accomplishments... up is the only direction. Those who stop, relax and take time out to think are the ones who care when silence is saying those who sit and write a letter to someone cares about what person think about them and the written subject. I feel annoyed, frustrated, aggravated for a reason I cannot comprehend. I am more because I can [not] figure out why.

What should I do to get rid of these negative feelings? I could go talk to someone until they have to do their own time, I could go and watch T.V. and try to forget, I can do the workout I planned, or I could just lie down and drown in my own thoughts. Yes, that is it.

2/11/17

I was just wondering how I would express my good-bye to those that helped me through this journey. Be going home or transferring to another camp, I may never see these people again. Some I have seen on a daily basis for years. I have been encouraged by, have encouraged, have taken advice, and learned a great deal from. This has been my home and the men here with me, my family. Some have left before me; some will leave though, the majority will never leave physical imprisonment.

2/11/17

This key is for the huge and minute things that insure our survival and is used to cope with each other and ourselves. We use it in attempt to manipulate, knowing and sometimes unknowingly, communication functions in a give and take way; something given, something received. This is such a broad subject so I will only touch on aspects close to me.

One huge way we communicate in our everyday life as inmates is pressing emergency buttons. Sometimes, we have to further communicate after the buttons are pressed; other times we do not.

When pressing the button we may rarely think about the wiring in which the electrons travel to get to the computer, then the noise it makes and then the officer reacting to the noise. In addition, pressing another button.

While on the subject of receiving, I will like to tell you about a conversation I had with my mother last Sunday about my sister…My mother repeated[ly] said that she was talking to my sister trying to help her out with life, yet she do not listen and is making the mistakes my mother made in the past. After saying one too many times that, my sister does not listen, I asked what she talks about. Communication should be two way, though many times its just one. Small communicative things like tucking in our shirts. A tucked shirt communicates several things: many more than I can and will like to touch on here. It communicates rule abiding, lowering our chances of being messed with by officers. I remember yesterday tucking in my shirt, telling myself, "Tuck in my shirt so this officer won't say anything to me." There is a key communication key that I take very serious, that many around me take for granted.

2/12/17

On a Sudoku puzzle, one never approach the puzzle knowingly a mindset to just place numbers in whichever spot you think is necessary will never suffice though we take our time to observe, analyze and evaluate the correct placements.

Each number has already been assigned to a specific spot there are no tricks or maneuvers needed to complete the puzzle you must only bring patient observation skills to complete the task ahead, and a little determination.

2/15/17

I know of a couple of millionaires, though I do not remember them giving me any advice on making millions, the long way and keeping them. Obviously, you would have to save more than you spend. You must purchase assets and not liabilities. You must constantly remember the long-term goal and not short. Your surrounding cast must be where you wish to get.

2/18/17

I would guess that dying is a tough thing it—when it is not instant and you are not expecting it. I would think especially when one feels that they have not accomplished and/or done enough. Though every single person should come to grips with dying because it is inevitable, rather its quick or slow, painful or soothing, it will come. I am thinking of many of what ifs. What if I die before I get released from prison, or the first day, week, month, or year after getting released? I think that will suck, though I will surely take that above living the rest of my life in prison. The next question is would I be mourned and if so for how long and by how many?

Who will remember me as a mature man instead of a playful kid? Those who have seen what I have grown into are all in prison with me, and have not chosen, themselves, to be a part of my life though is forced to. If they had the chance not to be a part of my life, it is likely they would not. When I am gone, another will take my place. I will then be forgotten in some, the process of seeing, retaining, remembering then forgetting is a never-ending cycle. The less we see of something, the more and faster we forget which is out of sight out of mind. My mother told me in the county jail at the beginning of this long though very short journey. Most inmates' family members probably do not even think of them dying in prison, failing to realize how unstable this environment is. If one of us suddenly die, one who has been discussing their release plan, goals and future with their family, most times than not the family members will be regretful, thinking that it was something they should have done or/and said more. I have replayed a family member's death multiple times and had to force myself on those occasions to not respond off the wall, yet accept that it is a part is life, and add it to the reasons why I should not have came to prison and reasons why not to come back, time constantly move if we're moving or not.

Later

Ideal vs real - there is a large amount of inmates that are not what their loved ones outside think they are.

These inmates make up all kinds of reasons why there family or friends should send them money; they join programs and go to church to put on a front as though they are doing the right thing. I must consider though those like myself, who talks the talk hoping to get out and walk the walk. I have forced myself to think, if it's true or not, that it is acceptable to act certain ways in prison that I would not dare act outside. My excuse is that inside and outside is two different worlds; possible in one may not be in the other. It is very amusing to think that I will live by and only accept a higher standard once I am released. I want and will pursue things, which most people do not even dream of. What I prefer has risen only because I have come to prison. The amusement is that what is available has lessened and/or will be more difficult for me to grasp because of my prison time. Everything from family, money, jobs, lovers, friends, goals, adventures.

23/17

To my sisters: Laying on the bunk while I am locked down, I have no television to watch to occupy my mind, no radio to distract me. I am left with white walls, my own thoughts, memories and dreams to keep me company. I am at peace knowing that I may get another chance to be a present brother, uncle, son, cousin, etc. I am [at] peace knowing that you will know my goals and aspirations to share them with me. I am at peace if I try them and accomplish my goals, or try to fail. The peace is here because my goals are set and I have planned;

I can only do what I can do.

Coming to prison has opened my mind, though I am unable to travel far physically, my horizons have been broadened. The unknown has become my limit. I want millions of dollars. I want to travel, see new things and have adventures. It took me to tear myself down to realize I had no foundation. I will be released as an ex-prisoner and sex offender to hold for the rest of my life. However, I will use these titles as fuel and my experience as my vehicle.

2/24/17

"The abundance of water thins and dilutes the blood". The analogy is as ABSOLUTE as the living body has flowing blood and is sustained by water. This is close to the friend or foe entry. Our families become strangers and strangers become family, as we grow old–out to find a mate– we learn everything we can about the prospect.

2/26/17

Why the sex offender chronicles? I feel as though there is a need to show that we are not all abominations. As every living and dead person have done, we made mistakes, however more severe, it is a mistake that can be learned from and growth being the effect. We are humans, we have family that we wish safe, and we will love to live in peace–some in private, some in public. We have been judged and sentenced a sentence we will be reminded of constantly for the rest of our lives.

*3/2/17

I placed a star in front of this entry because it is an umbrella goal that I have that will take precedence over most others.

Why do I want to be a millionaire?

-Why not? No reason unless I'm incapable

-Because I know no one personally, that has become a millionaire from the bottom through business ventures, collaborating and managing their money.

- My immediate family deserves the sacrifice
- I'm willing to sacrifice

I have seen myself with nothing when wanting; I would like to need not, nor want any material thing without being able to get it. I would like to see my money work harder than I do, and make more money than I do.
I would like the money strain eliminated in my immediate family. The test is to have more needing less I will pass the test; most fail.

For some reason I thought to write up this "agreement" and while writing I have been thinking it up, I take full responsibility for my actions and isolation from the free society. I do not doubt that I am now made a target. I wish to be passed over by the mendacious and malevolent and constantly in the sights of the gracious and benevolent ones.

This is to protect myself from the unseen conjuring, because that which, whom, and or what I see and know I will be able to escape the cunning devices. If you have read this, are still in pursuit, and are of age, I will assume you a benefactor and or sponsor of my endeavors.

3/5/17

"The example of patient suffering is in itself the most precious of all lessons to an impatient world".

3/6/17

"We first get hurt and begin trying to cover up, protect ourselves growing up confused, angry, hurt, wounded, afraid, resentful, after assuming we have been protecting ourselves, we realize that we can't; we are the last source of protection. There are others around who may be able to help, though well-guarded, well-intended conspiracy of silence surrounds almost every conversation. "When life is moving fast and in a straight line, it's easy to discount anything slow and circular."

"I have cried again, I don't remember the last time I cried, maybe when I apologized for my ignorance to Christopher Hickman and Darrel Morgan, though I am not sure." The reason I cried was because a better truth I was writing to my mother, the truth that those who I see as my family are strangers and those who are strangers has the role of my family, I am only tolerated in prison for temporary pleasure.

Who am I to those who only have seen me in blue and n prison or to those that have not experienced my growth by my side? The important unseen, that is part of me, is only a figment to others.

3/8/17

"Integrity is admitting what you can do, and doing what you can."
It is crazy after so long. In addition, reading one book–me being molested is likely or most surely the start of my descent thirteen years later. I only remember seeing it as a small occurrence. Something that was embraced and tainted as a child this was a significant event, an event I must hide from as I grew older–my shield grow thicker, and the event was remembered less, I begin to feel less shameful and tainted. My self-protection felt more secure. Why should I tell people so they could feel bad for me and I seem weak? Have something for them to bring to the table– Against me; with that said knowledge, I believe that I have taken a step forward. I have walked miles both backward and forward.
Though I truly believe, I am now headed in the right direction.

3/9/17

We who have harbored the shame for so long does not ask…not expect pity, with our disclosure we gladly embraced the freedom.
Relationship as the stranger becomes the family–as two become one. I believe I have to write this down now. As if it is a plan, I wish not to fail to plan, and have some sort of warning to one who wishes to become family. Everyone says, or most, a foundation must be laid

and had for anything to be built with meaning and last. Though to be different, I have thought about a process which is unknown by many and is detrimental to the lasting of the foundation and structure above. This is the process of curing the ground that the foundation would be laid upon. The process that ensures longevity of the foundation, making sure the earth beneath does not shift and destroy the somewhat solid structures above.

3/25/17

the curing or injection of sort is this plan. Trust is going to be worked on and developed. How can I trust that the opposite sex will trust me wholeheartedly after me being in this situation; while I am a forever sex offender? I would wish to know everything about my mate and I will want them to know all about me. We are together–out [our] past, present and future, we so things now because we have learned from our experienced behind us and or what we wish to experience ahead. To know ones past, another can gauge their present state to together improve the future. An open mind is being able to move with the tide, though never forgetting how to swim (holding fast to morals and principles). Despite that which is contrary to plan for the future holding wanted and unwanted circumstances not to be guarded though prepared. What if a job is lost, what if one gets sick. A house gets broken down; a family member is hospitalized, even imprisoned. A trip comes up, a good property foresees, an investment opportunity is revealed or comes through.

Money and a desire or willingness or composure or self-restrain must be had and thought upon and ready to act.

4/10/17

On the weekend of the first of this month, the gang and I had strawberry cheesecake that I wish to save the recipe of it and others:

- 1 cheese squeeze
- 4 3oz peanut butter

2 smashed strawberry pop tarts
- 15 Oreo cookies
- 15 vanilla cookies
- 20 creamers
- 20 1 tablespoon creamers

Saw live statue and I wish to take my own live statue pictures, have someone paint me the color of bronze or copper statue and pose while someone take the pictures. I want to have Photoshop though use it as less as possible.

4/11/17

Because of the loss of license and being an inexpensive way to move around, electric scooters are very advantageous. You may buy five for $300 each then sell them for a profit. This method can be applied with multiple products.

4/14/17

How can I encourage one who got it worst than I; have been through experiences that exceeds the amount of years they and I have lived upon this earth. Though it seems impossible, I have to try–it must be explained even though your situation seems terrible and unjustifiable…yours is not the worst of them though you are seen as a common criminal, living among them and sharing thoughts and dreams with them. You do not have to succumb to the foolish ways of the majority. Imagine or even think of what is likely to be true; the innocent being raped, murdered, convicted then sentenced to life incarceration for something or someone they had no dealings with. If you are able to, discern and rationalize; you are a strong one that will be able to survive. One able to adjust and adapt to things that only can become justifiable through your acceptance of your inevitable. You are one of the greats. Why are you here now? If you could have known how to handle the situations that lead you to prison, wouldn't you want to know…why not be an example spreading the knowledge of "prison prevention," to the future? We now find ourselves in a place that we rather not are, though, where else can we be? We can work to be somewhere better in the future, though our present is here, we can only make what is now beneficial to our future.

4/27/17

"Doing No to Recidivism" Introduction: What I Now [know], currently in prison, feels like I have to do to stay out of prison.

Number 1: As a sex offender, my first is to know and abide by all of the registration rules. I have accepted that I am a sex offender and there is not legal way, if I would like to stay in United States, to resist, unless I wish to come back to prison, which [I] do not!

4/28/17

Number 2: Talking to Reginald luster yesterday. I retold my past and saw my past while talking. I saw that once I removed myself from the college athlete, I had no friends. I had no one to spend time with on a level that was close to mine. The males I was close to played football and may have lived in a different area (likely lived in a different area)…the female I was close to, was not close to at all; though saw them as only a "hookup". I have opened up to my family to hopefully be able to have them feel the friendship spot, my brother will be a main player if I can find a common group.

I have gone nearly five years without sex, I know now I can make it. Having had no close intimate relationship with the opposite sex other than my family, has proven to me that I can hold on until the correct female comes along.

Number 3: Helping others less fortunate: fortune may be physical, mental or "spiritual". One aspect that will show me (remind) the things that I took for granted. The things that I thought important are nothing at all when it came to "my" happiness; while helping others, I mainly help myself. "Nothing I do is not beneficial to me."

Number 4: I must look at the big picture. All who and what I am associated with most be worth the connection and by all circumstances, must be worth the connection and by all circumstances, must not risk my life nor freedom. The instant satisfaction is irrelevant, the long run and lasting affect is what matters the most. From buying a new gadget to choosing a sexual partner.

1, 2, 3 & 4: staying connected to some of the dudes that I met in prison. Some of them will or are going to experience the same things I will when I am released. I am sure to be reminded by the people that nothing is worth coming back to prison. Though they may have some time on their sentence, I am sure encouragement will be plentiful...our connection with that which may be the toughest thing a lot can go through; we went through prison together; my letters will be very helpful to many, including myself, showing that I have been touched and formed somewhat by the connection I had with the individuals I write. Most times we as prisoners force ourselves to look at one day at a time. Though as the sentence becomes short, we must consider where each day compiled will lead us. Knowing we are taking one step at a time, making sure we do not trip over an obstacle and fall. The destination which every single step together will lead is just as important.

Number 5: I wish to expect anything from grown "established" people, expect the worst, or nothing at all. Having integrity is the main goal for yourself; enter cleanness and openness no matter how dirty surrounding situations and people are.

5/12/17

I thought about this theory multiple times, though it seems I have alluded to writing it down. Some may think it an excuse and others an explanation. I believe my reasoning for creating this theory is to give the forgetful, truth breakers and liars an excuse.

As humans we surround ourselves with people or things we can relate to, or to fill some sort of empty void. In prison, some inmates get closer to others and fill some of the emptiness. We may get real close and personal sharing thought and secrets–shedding blood and tears. Sometimes this closeness is intentional for either vile or honest reasons. However, sometimes it's circumstances that brings us together...based on this connection we choose our closeness. Too Much

When we leave prison, the voids must be filled again. Replaced out the emptiness is easily replaced and what was substituted by the circumstances of prison now has returned. It is determined by our view of prison, to have us wish to remember or forget our connections in prison. It's determined by our sincerity on if we

decide to stay connected to that which saved our lives or someone else's.

The saving may not be life or death...it can be ignorance or a displacement for ignorance.

8/1/17

The process or the results/ the body or the conclusion...-which is more important to you: where you are going or how you get there? It is difficult for me to discuss this subject objectively without taking the side that I believe is more important, with my limited knowledge, even though I may be able to explain, argue or dispute with what I may consider common sense, I will not be supported by unlimited facts. This creates a dilemma such as "which came first, the chicken or the egg." As I can argue for one side, the opposite side is argued for, just as adamant. Some think that the process is the important piece, though just as many explains the result. The process is nothing, once you have completed the task or have failed, the way is irrelevant. However, there may be just as many individuals that gives credence equally to both integers. ABSOLUTE TRUTH is of all opinions with and without discrepancy.

8/10/17

Rather be the foe or the friend- it's hard sometimes to think that being close and open with some people is better than being far and closed to them.

Being close, one is expected to act and think a certain way. One even may be seen as obligated to respond certain ways and act at certain times that are not in tuned with one's current feelings.

Sometimes, it is detrimental to be inconsistent or unsure. That is unsolved in turn when close to someone, it lessens the expectations that they have; diminishing the strain of possible failure. And letting another down...Absolute forces are ever changing. There are both pushing and pulling, tensions and releasing... present all around at all times. We shall not succumb totally to no one force.

8/16/17

Incorporating a single tendency into lifestyle- when one have decided to change a part of their life for the better this part must be visualized then incorporated to every part of their life. The change in one particular must be compatible to all phases of life.

8/20/17

I wish to be called "The Sex Offender" because there is no positive thoughts that begin when one hear's someone is a sex offender, all are negative. I don't wish people to think positive thoughts, however, have an open mind when they come in contact with a sex offender. Safe guards must be in place with sex offenders, yet, they also should with any stranger. I may state with confidence that sex offenders are doing time by being constantly monitored by registration. There are some things sex offenders can not do, or must follow certain guidelines in which others don't see.

Because of the classification of "Sex Offender," there is a stigma, stereotype and discrimination. Sex offenders are sentenced to, sometimes prison, for the rest of their lives. Those discouraging things, most of the times, encourages sex offenders to live in secret. Their information is public, so sex offenders wish to live in secret. They attempt to stay under the radar as much as possible, hopefully. Many times, confidence is lost or it never has a chance to be developed, because of the sex offender status. Most people wish to be defined by what they do, not what they have done. Being one of the few sex offenders who will publicize my mistakes, though also show how I have learned from them.

I will live as a civil citizen, and know, the cause and effect of the violation of the sexual battery statute has been thoroughly considered, has been view…the crime has been replayed. A conviction was sought and found, then comes the sentence to be served. The purpose is victim prevention, recidivism prevention, prison prevention; the reason is to be aware of the normal Lifestyles that are alive today…observing the frequency, it seems as though immeasurable Lifestyles is…long for matters is that one has brought pain to multiple individuals in wish to make others aware of the warning signs and actions that has become an epidemic on the college campus

5/29/17

I wish to write about my Foolish Pride...something that I must work on that which I thought was not necessary.

5/22/17

Well before then because I was speaking recklessly to my roommate...talking about getting him moved out of the room for some reason or another...I don't like him out of my way to tell him I was oh I couldn't live go on Monday the 22nd...bold and called him a coward and told him he had low self-esteem and I didn't like his Ora...who it was around 6 in the morning about 15 minutes before I headed to school. I entered the building again at around the afternoon and was told I was moved to be for team...I knew it was in relation to my statements that morning though...I wish not to believe them

10/20/17

A few days later, another situation...it began when I started working...poking at a co-worker for coming when he want it and not teaching when needed to express his dislike for the job and camp and I express my dislike in him...how long for 2 or 3 days a week for about 3 months...one Monday in late May, when our teacher was absent, he touch my cup and we began to argue...so I won't be out to cool off about the situation, he came in and asked for scores of the students test...angry expressing my dislike of him and his methods, he finally stated that he didn't care for any inmate...forget us...that I will come see him...this is from the conversations I've been having lately with my clothes Associates...subjects such as there are many good dudes in prison I believe or me issues has to think that there is not as many good dudes in prison as it is said to be in prison removes key responsibilities...those responsibilities in which probably need them to present...this is what makes an assisted transition necessary for those coming out of prison...one must get back adjusted to the stresses of outside life and which are not possible in prison bills dealing with family, availability of drugs and alcohol, when these stress is hitting all cylinders...those are the situations and circumstances that Define if a person is truly a good dude

10/24/17

I went back and forth with myself asking should I say something or not about earlier...I decided to because I care and I know that are grown man; we ourselves control [our]on Destiny's; yes I am here to teach and you are here to learn...the question is are to be given something or are you all here to earn something?

10/25/17

I am standing here today to learn or receive a small version of speaking to the masses...that we have grown...fight the eyes...despite law enforcement placing us where it was meant only to punish yet we have rehabilitated ourselves...come a voice for those who can make something out of just an opportunity and the resources; be someone or a group to breed down our next or hold our hands man–we are leaders and mentors...be released today...enjoy the legitimate Workforce supporting ourselves and our families–mentally, spiritually and financially; to preach– no, give you anything...you know I came to this job from scratch though, I was willing to put much in understanding that all would get out of it was the intangible.

10/26/17

The sex offender who's ever determine sold help ex felons get back on their feet assist and Community projects...Mentor those in need of positive counsel other sex offenders mentally restless and...

11/7/17

I had a dream that showed me at a retreat of some sort. I was ordered to crawl only with my hands and arms. I was going slow at first then someone advised me to speed up my pool to not let my food settle in my stomach...he said it in a Zen way–my voice–it was probably my voice. I see myself throwing my mother a party to remember or having a gathering in which I will spoil her...example of why it is great to be alive at 50, a half a decade... she will and all of us will know what success its– freedom...fierce...

frustration...fierce...inferior...sears...fierce...failure...success...
memes...respect...continually finding more real happiness and
satisfaction from life for those who depend on you as a family
being successful; we will be if the family believe that we will

11/13/17

I think the perpetrator will be better than the sex offender because
I am representing multiple crimes it does fashion down enough to
start a conversation.

11/14/17

Palmetto Georgia was a hardware store that starts off people in
landscaping business to build one or two more houses on the
property then I maintenance.

11/15/17

An image of me 10 years from now work departments: years
from now come level 2 of responsibility: do I see how much
authority? do I want to command for...what do I expect to gain from
my work; home Department...10 years from now...one: what kind
of standard of living do I want to provide for my family and myself;
two: what kind of house do I want to live in; three: what kind of
vacations do I want to take; four: what do I want to give my children
and their early adult years? social Department: 10 years from now,
what kinds of friends do I want to have to what social groups? Do I
want to join 3...what community leadership positions Would I like to

hold for what worthwhile causes? Do I want to Champion 30- day Improvement guy?

12/15/ 17

I will break these habits 1: things; 2: negative language; 3: watching TV more than 60 minutes per day…for gossip, acquire these habits: 1. morning nation of my parents clan each day's work the night before compliment people at every possible opportunity increase my value to my employer and these ways: one- do a better job of developing my subordinates; to- about my company, make suggestions for efficiency…be value to my home; show more appreciation for the little things; to- do something special weekly; 1 hour daily to family; in my mind, invest 2 hours daily to reading professional magazines, one self-help book…make for new friends…30 minutes quiet time.

12/14/17

I thought about OOSOOM: out of sight out of mind…just thinking about they are going to do it because I am not around to ask or end see me at all.

1/10/18

Most or all of my interest are in my diary…the book with the

purpose; then, I began to read and let thought… once I read my entry from the 27th of November, I remember 4 first letters sent out of prison to my mother was to let her know that I wished for close mentally and spiritually no matter how far we are away from each other physically… we, that we are okay and are not forgotten…feel this way with the guys I'm close to in here…religion barring.

1/11/18

I feel as though I have to find other possible names that will also play in the cold or mission of what began as back Academy 1; making a change; 2: cm-changing Minds; 3: cam- changing a mind; 4: CAD- changing a dynamic; 5: reversal of revolving experience door roared January 13th 2018…FPTS movement from perpetrator to savior or preventer 718 2018- offender turns Defender

A procession of pictures with sculptures

From the mind to the actual picture place the camera within the picture

1/15/18

And isolation in silence while the body rest, the spirit wishes to expand through the Mind's acceptance.

1/17/18

A 3D printer will be a great investment.

1/31/18

Jerome page

Her only stated that a mistake was something you have done and if you can go and [in] the past and change it, you will; that's an

action that one regrets.

I was corrected today: something one do not mean to do is a mistake; I did not know… this apologize for my reaction made you back off and not even attempt direct me many terms and sometimes common knowledge has missed the mark…my strength is that I am willing to learn from this place, actions and thoughts.

1/30/18

What have you learned in prison assignment for COC?

No Date

I learned that I was not alone in this world also that I was not in the best situation but I definitely not in the worst situation…matter where I am physically or financially, my mind can open up to my spirit becoming free, rich and satisfied.

No Date

I realize my potential and establish proper expectations. I set goals created through correct principles and values because of our unique human endowments, new programs for ourselves, totally apart from our past culture experience, instincts and training.

No Date

Time to plan to get out I begin and come to the conclusion that I will do the time. I will send it to my occupations are limited being a sex offender, yet, being a sex offender created and enormous amount of opportunities for me and amount that would to entertain them all.

Later- 1-31-18

TOBA- the other business attire

2/20/18 C.O.C. assignment

The subjects are placed in an order that one has to transition to the first one before the other to be entertained before the next thoughts lead to actions (behavior) then tested and developed more.

My thinking goal is to be positive, progressive, productive and palpable. I must be proactive...reaching my thinking goal every moment of every day. if I am not feeling positive, I must figure out what is making me feel otherwise and work to change it; this method helps me to continually progress and not regress…mentally productive thinking is creative planning. Making things happen and getting things done.

A most important step is placing people around me with similar goals. A person is the mirror image of the top 5 people they are seen with most. I understand that some of my thoughts may not be aligned with my goals. So I must stay palpable. Taking personal inventory and being willing to listen to the advice of the great people in my circle of influence.

All behavior and actions began as a thought, as the saying goes "think it, feel it, do it." So my main goal for my behavior characteristics is they, they exude my thoughts. My thinking goals are my main values and principles to have long lasting values, principles and relationships– they must be freely chosen, prized and cherished, publicly and privately proclaimed and acted on continually.

I wish for my education and employment to be life sustainingfrom thoughts to actions to developing (education) those thoughts then implementing (employment, family, friends, etc.) them. I see life or living as being in a classroom, inside, r outside a physical classroom. I will continue my education to better the way I live every day. I will be willing to explore a broad spectrum of people and places.

3/7/18

Outside or external things that I put too much weight on can be triggers which play against my positivity.

I have come to understand myself in a deeper sense, realizing the way I respond to in a very inappropriate way. I expected another human to basically react to me, my presence, to have goals that I expected. When they did not, I felt cheated and that I wasted my time. With that person, I lashed out in hopes to correct them.

A less traumatic occurrence recently happened when an acquaintance lied to me about something trivial. I became upset because I expected more from the person and my expectations were not even considered. I went on a ridiculous binge to calm down and get my mind off the situation.

A preventative measure is to never think that a person will not let me down. It is always possible, no matter how tuned I think we are mentally, physically and/or spiritually.

I can only lessen the perception by being open to communication with the person(s). Know their goals, values and principles and knowing their willingness to live by their word.

Letting myself down is a trigger for negative thinking as well. I look back now and see how I can be very emotionally dependent.

Knowing and realizing I have let another person control my thinking is very disappointing. To think one person or even a group of people has to be a part of my life does not give up with my values, principles and goals.

I must be able to function after losing a piece I considered at the time significant.

It is crucial for me to have someone or multiple people who I can trust and feel comfortable talking about anything without the judgement pressure hanging over my head. I also must have an outlet; going to work out, walk or just going to see a movie will be a part of my regular routine, just to wind down and re-center.

3/16/18

How can I replace my negative triggers with a positive mindset? My triggers are, to my understanding, external things, being let down by others or letting down myself...to replace these triggers...must first identify what they are.

If its money- I will recent [resent] myself realizing that I am probably not managing my money effectively.

If people- I hope and will look forward to establishing relationships that have open lines of communication to solve any problems.

If myself; I will have a set time when I take inventory of my actions and feelings: looking back to get the reasons I may have felt negative or did something that was not aligned with my main goal then correct it so that it will not happen in the future. I wish to have people that feel comfortable correcting me.

If I am just overwhelmed with what seems to be everything, I will have some sort of close body of water to go swim in to just decompress.

I love to be totally submerged in water. Feeling free, and limitless, serene, tranquil and positivity at its best.

3/23/18- 4/4/18

I see myself free on April 2023 married for at least three years, waking up every day beside someone I chose to cherish, and they me. I will be a solid structure my family can depend on. I will be well known in my community for lending a helping hand when needed. My job will be one that energizes me, not break me down.

To first obtain then continue to have a loving family, believe positivity is vital I may fail to meet Miss Right after several attempts though keeping the attitude that it will happen is a positive one and one that will help me succeed in that aspect.

A solid structure to depend on is not limited to physical. It includes mental and emotional (spiritual). When things get bad, everyone must be reminded that it can be worse and single events do not make or break. We cannot control what or who act toward us, but we can control how we respond to it.

I plan to make community service my occupation. Doing so will keep me grounded to my values, knowing that I do not have it bad, people are living in worse states (mentally). I will be a part of a circle who receives a livelihood through giving one.

4/5/18

My main value is happiness/positivity
I value progression. I believe as though life is the field for
growth whether mentally, emotionally or physically. Growth and
progress is the reason for living. Even if my story can help another
progress, I must tell it to the masses because it is my story given to
me by another. Family, I also value no matter through blood or
community, I believe in helping those I have a born connection with
or a developed mentality.

4/20/18 - 5/3/18

Things that I can do for my family and community:
I must first be an example of positivity. I can always show through
example that I am not what I have done wrong but I am defined by
my correct decisions and who I present myself as every moment
now. My family needs to begin to budget and start thinking ahead,
considering times and uncontrollable events. For my community, I
can help by giving my time to charitable [organizations] and
fundraisers. Being an example and hopefully starting a business to
create jobs and bring revenue to the community.

5/4/18

This is my second day on my detox and I am not as inspired as I
was at the beginning of my entries. I decided to drink water

because of the advice others gave me and the way I felt after the morning eating with Black. I feel tired and aggravated not really wanting to talk; I didn't teach the last two days. I do feel as though I can let go what people prize so much, my brother showed me yesterday that what others say of him apply to me as well… tough.

5/14/18

Black expressed the idea of a Florida event publication; where we take pictures of events held in Florida and make it into a magazine for people behind these walls…can "get out" for a few seconds.

5/15/18

How have I changed? There are only two people in my family that I can think of that I had a relationship with before coming to prison and continue to have one within prison now.

At first my mother had nothing but good to say. I had to remind her of my selfishness and secretive life I had been living. The misery I was feeling when I was out, when I was out, had never been fully disclosed or expressed to my family fully until I came to prison. I now feel, even though I have not lived it that I will be a more open person to the ones who are willing to live with the consequences of my actions. My sister had more to say, she recognized the change in me. She described me as more open and wanting to help others. She explains that it seems as though I have more plans thought out and able now to articulate them better. My brother was in prison for 5 years prior to my incarceration; I did have a strong relationship with my father or paternal father before coming to prison, so I talk to them now attempting to build a relationship before I get back out.

6/2/18 – 6/12/18

How am I going to get the precise training in the area I wish to work? I basically answered this last meeting with the print outs I received from multiple teachers. I would need a master's degree in counseling. Training (on the job) is required for most degree programs in the fields; building a network consisting of several therapists/counselors with their own practices and or support/ interest groups. I may even join a group to understand the ends and outs of it while receiving pertinent information on myself.

6/30/18

I dreamt of a young female wanting me though I held her off and asked for her to give it a years' time then the thought may be reconsidered. Not that I wanted to run wild, though I would have wanted her to find a worthier mate, who will have no doubt in his mind of a true commitment.

Ever since I have been reading "The Brand Within", I have been thinking of a job of being a Brand Coach. I Give advice to people on how to market themselves to reach the goals they are willing to sacrifice for Contentment = consuming time.

7/3/18

From the start of the day there was greatness present. Black and I talked of our past dealings with law enforcement and much came out in the sense of bitterness and getting over it. The way we must place ourselves in their shoes came up in the conversation…I moved alone with Barkley…also not allowing someone to be in control of our life in a way we can control.

7/16/18

I wrote my sister today and wanted to copy something from the letter:

Integrity: being the same on scene and off

Honesty: telling and living by truth even if it hurts

Love: forgiving those closest and furthest away from my life's mission

Progress: moving forward on all endeavors; from relationships to working out

Dependability: What I say I'm going to do, what I know I have to do, will be done

Open Minded: If one thinks they are right and correct, they are.

LIVE THE WAY I THINK AND BELIEVE IS CORRECT UNLESS PROVEN OTHER WISE

8

JOURNALING BEYOND BARS

The below journal entries were made during my first 27 days after being released. I hope that my sharing of these entries will help you better understand the challenges and the day-to-day life of someone transitioning from prison life. (Journal entries for Days 28-63 are available in the back of the book.)

First 27 out:

8/28/18 – 8/31/18

The day came and went and on a positive, not I only can say that I got the introduction out of the way. With mother, sister, granddad, dad, nieces and nephew, Harry and the one and only Mark-e-Mark. It's crazy how much I want to be done and do not know the first thing I am going to do. Begin to provide for my family. I know that there is only one way I must go through and that is up. From helpless to helpful. I am told to sit back and let things come together for me. That is easier said than done. Well, I do have the job on the weekend to be done. My, I do not– will not– want the people to think I let them down so I must send at least a couple of letters back in to be in contact.

That will relieve some of my pressure. Honesty, Integrity, Love, Progress Everyday.

Well it has been a journey and thinking about it now I am scared, I really do not know what they (my registration people) have missed and/or what I truly have to do with my registration. I don't want to go to the office and get picked up for something that I slipped and didn't even know that I had to do then get sentenced to the highest extent. I have been interacting with my brother as though I'm a stickler for the laws and not truly knowing if I'm doing the correct things or not.

I was told that Georgia has become the toughest on sex crimes in the U.S. and I do not want to be caught in their web. I have read letters from Barkley, Spivey, Black and Nuckles though have missed placed the others inside the pile of stuff that have met me in the room I was assigned. Housework has accumulated and I have got absent minded. I have not worked out nor have I been neither drinking water, as I should nor meditating properly.

I will go see my people today just so I could let them know what have been going on; I had to take both the written (computer) test and the driving test to get my driver's license because my license had expired 3 months too late. I got my F.S.U. email back up and Guess now I am a fan. I do not have a phone number yet, but my dad is talking of, or stated that he would get me a phone, and hopefully pay the bill, until I get right.

Another thing I have been getting up early since my release and staying up working in the yard, or getting things, (paperwork) completed. I must keep in mind that I must register everything that changes with me to the office (that was type of a reminder to me). I have to let them know what car I am driving (none are mine though I am may drive it), I have to see them today.

Now I must say that it is now 3:28 in the morning. I have been up almost an hour now, do not know when I went to sleep last night. I planted greens yesterday morning with my mom, which was exciting. I do not have any social media account as of this moment so I asked my mother to post a picture of the 277-collared green plants we planted yesterday. We have to go out and maintain it constantly though I will see how that is when and if I am not hauled away to prison or jail today (scary) but true. I am trying to write a catch all letters to all that I have stated I will and if anyone ask if you got a letter, or have heard from me, please let them read this. I do not have a printer at this moment, or do not have ink or internet to print or even, well I do not want to write this out though

I will let some individuals know that this is coming within the next month or so and I will keep it updated as my laziness and focus permits. I must turn my words into works; I must and I know this.

I have been down with and Love you people...black's letter was the most touching to me as of now. Well I could erase that and say that all of them touch me as it is but that one I let my mother and brother (yes, my brother I have not seen since 2007) read, to boost my spirit and let them know and hopefully understand and agree with my Life's goal now. My brother is as crazy as I have talked about he was, though he has stayed and spent time with me since I have been out and I love his craziness more for that, even though I have to walk away from it at times.

It is currently the 31st my mother's b-day was yesterday and all I had the ability was time to give her, I hope that was enough. Which brings me to the point that this is not easy though it is defiantly [definitely] not as hard as many because I do not have to struggle for the necessities many or most have to get out of prison and face? Meaning that I should not have to look back and say if I'm doing the correct thing or not with my sex offender registration or not, like I said I will do it no matter how confusing and conflicting my thoughts, the law and my investigators view of the law my seem. I have to do what the law says while appeasing my investigator.

Now let me tell you of the first meeting with my investigator. I went in with a hat that I hop[e] for you all to see a picture of that I sported my first and second day. Scratch that you all will see a picture of it; at the soonest, I get to Wal-Mart with my mother to print the pictures out. I will let you all know if and when I will get a social media so that if possible you all will let your families and friends travel with me, just ask them to friend request me, everything will be public so that they will be able to see. Now even they can request my mother at Cynthia Harris in Albany, Georgia on Facebook. In addition, when I send pictures, please share them with those who ask and/or you may think will like to see.

I had to remind myself on the 2nd day out, the journey is a marathon not a sprint. I have the ability to look around while jogging seeing and maneuvering in response to my surroundings and opponents (obstacles). Thinking about social media when and if I get it up, I would like to post when I being responded by my brothers behind bars to push some awareness…I will even drop your jewel if you wish, so let me know if you would not like to be a part of that, no response means you are fine with it.

Those who are in the same quad, I will only send one letter so please pass this around to those who ask about me and/or those you think will like to read this. It is a lot here, I am only a millionaire in mind at this moment and paper, and ink is a tough right now. That's all for now and I might send this out alone so you all

STAY STRONG, POSITIVE, LOVING AND PEACEFUL
TO THOSE AROUND YOU, BUT FIRST TO YOURSELF

8/31/18

My mother and I was out from about nine until 4:15 getting things done, and boy it was a lot of driving. Again, I woke up at 2:30ish and now I am tired. My brother fixed the A.C. or just actually looked within the unit at the breakers, and then look to what was needed, while at Lowes I asked for fuses I meant, that was 200,000 volts. Shows how much I remember from electrical class. Soon as we got back, I remembered the Cakery and the need to go, so we jumped right back inside the truck to go. At the cakery, I ate most of my mother's cookie, which she did not like over the much cheaper 'Wal-Mart brand. Getting back Harry supposed to show, so when hearing the revving of a truck I surly thought it was Harry though it was Ms. Tora wanting her greens. She even gave my mother some to finish off her garden. Therefore, Harry and I finished off the 100 or so plants that were left.

9/1/18

Yesterday I was so tired and, busy– better to say occupied that I did not type, I grabbed the computer and had the intentions to but my sister brought my flash dive that she had for the time I've been down and I wanted to see if it worked and the things I left on it. The day begin with me getting up first at three then hoping 5, but I slept until seven and had to take my mother the bad news because we had planned on getting up with the sun to make it to the flea market. We parachuted out of the bed to make it as soon as we could.

My brother Mark decided that he did not want to stay in for the day so he decided to drive the car to the flea market directly after us, catching us then leaving us. We got ice then made our way to the flea market. There were many people there and it was great for me to get into some conversation and speak with people. I felt the feeling that nothing slowed down and jumped directly back into life, without missing a beat, no one cared that I came out of prison or was a sex offender…they went on…people went on with their lives. We had juices, water and sodas and they went great because it got hot. My mother explained to me what she wanted to do and I am all aboard when it comes to, making a good living, and giving people what they think they want to spend their money on. Harry also stated that he was in the running for getting a contract for cutting and maintaining the lawns of six waffle houses, and would not mind if I worked for him.

I hoped as soon as I heard, if that can be the great break that I need to get going in the right direction. When we finally made it home, it was somewhat late and Dellaina was not here yet, she had to get her oil changed in Tifton. There was only talk about who should cook and what not, so I decided to bunker down and do the Mac and cheese myself. It took me a while to get the stove ready, because I did not know how it worked. Once Dellaina came, I finally got it to work and the water to boil for the noodles. I did not know where the things were in the cabinets, so I had to constantly ask. I cleaned dishes as my sister and I cook, she cooked shrimp and rice, and fried the chicken alone while I did the mac and cheese. We both pitched in

119

to do the southern bake beans. Ta'ti made the cake mix to be put in the oven. The meal was great; Mumama, Mark, and most of the kids were out front playing. Once the food was done, everyone went outside and so the fun...Dellaina and I recorded the fun until everyone got tired and were ready to eat. Mark was ready to go because he could not make any money here and Albany. After eating, I bid my brother goodbye, but first we had to take a picture with him, because it is no telling; life happens.

9/2/18

I woke up on time on Sunday (9/2/18), around 4:30 and had to use the toilet twice before it was time to leave to go to the flea market. My mother and I went first to Wal-Mart to get some more drink, because they sold good the day before, then some ice to make sure they were cold. We were some of the first to arrive before the sun came up and the mosquitoes were there to let us know we did not belong. Both, my mother and me dressed bad, and had to change into clothes with sleeves. I spoke to most that came by, though we both became tired within a few hours. The drinks sold well because the sun made its way out in good time. Unlike the day before where my mom's things and the drinks did well, Sunday only the drinks did well. I had the intentions to go out and help Harry plant his greens though that did not work out because he had been busy all day with meetings and what not. After the flea market, nothing happened. Harry came later while it was a little sun light out though he said that

it would not be until the next day that we would get to plant the
greens

9/3/18

On Monday (Labor Day) I woke up at about 5:30 ready to go
though I know that I set my mother's clock at 6:00…so I ate, used
the toilet, then woke her up. However, she did not want to get up
until eight. Therefore, I out the door to do some yard work before
Harry came. My mother called him; however, he had to take his son
out to practice before he made it to my side, to pick my mother and
me up.

I transferred some broken branches to the junk pile and laid
some grits on ant piles before Harry came an hour later. Once I saw
him, I told him that I just was warming up. Once we got to the farm,
I had to encourage them to start, to hopefully get it done in one
swipe, after an hour and a half, mother had to take a break. We
drank water for our break then attempted to get back to it. This time
I gave out, got dizzy, and had to lie down because I know the feeling
of dehydration. That called for the last break and we went to
Subway and Dollar General to get some water. During our time at
Subway, I got a little mouthy at the cashier, though she was not in
the mood for the final hour of her shift. Harry really did not like that
that the female was becoming a little belligerent, and stated that it
happened because I was out of circulation for a while. Once we got
back, I wanted to get back started and finish, though it took about 15
minutes. We went for a while then my mother dropped off,

fortunately, Harry's son (Dave) came at the right time to help. It was good to meet him, though I can tell that he is not taking up his father's farming, We finished off in what I thought was another hour, however when it was done, 3 hours had elapsed. After the work, we went back to the house and nothing was planned so I went to take a shower and get ready for the day ahead. I bid everyone a good night then went to sleep at around 10:00pm.

9/4/18

Today, I woke up around the same time as yesterday but knew that mother did not want to get up to early, so I let her be. I knew that Kenni and I needed to get going [to] the job fair and only hoped that she would get up in time to feed her two kids and get dressed to go. We had to go by the library to print out our resumes, so there editing I did before leaving. Once we got to the library, I decided to get a card just in case I wanted to check out, or buy some books. Then we headed off to the job fair on time as I said it. At 2:30 pm, no one was around to let us inside the Civic Center to get started. A little before the start time, three, the organizer begin to show up. Kenni and I was not in the right place so there were people just arriving getting in line before us. We met one of Kenni's classmates from Elementary who showed us the ropes and Kenni and I talked to [him] during our wait. He was a person with a destination without a route, so I attempted to encourage him as much as possible. The interviewers called then interviewed in a span of 5 minutes, which could have been good or bad. Kenni was waiting 2 hours after me and I had to speak to multiple people before she was finally seen and told that her application was lost. Once we finished, we made a trip to the post office so that I could drop off some letters, then we headed home. While at the house, I was beat and did not want to do anything, so that is exactly what I did. Now, it's time to lay it down and look forward to the next day. It is now 9:50 and I am currently up to date with my journal. TIL NEXT TIME.

9/5/18

I woke up with the sun today as I have been doing since I have been out. The difference from the other days and today is that I got up and cleaned a lot of the junk that is in the room I am currently sleeping in. I decided to stretch for the first time since I have been out, not the first time but a focused stretch that gets the mind right. I also meditated on the day ahead and the days pass, with passivity and peaceful thoughts and memories. I thought of my brothers down and hope that they are doing as well as they can be in the circumstances they are in. Good and bad in every aspect of this life, however, to deem them all good and/ or neutral will give me a step ahead of those struggling with demons as Jay explained to me yesterday. My mother asked me to cook for her and I really did not feel like it for many reasons, though I must remember that without her I would be probably stressing out right now. Therefore, I did the grits, eggs and sausages thing.

On a side note: For those that will one day get out and/or advising someone that will get out, I don't know how strenuous it would have been without my family with me. I do not have any money, no job, no vehicle, though I am still making it and do not have to worry about much of the things I would have had to make necessities. Therefore, my advice is for you all to stay or get close to those who supposed to love you the most. Also, save as much money as possible; so you may have spending money, or those who are taking care of you, just give it all to them. Bills will pile up, I have been out 9 days and bills are accumulating.

Well I got a call to go fill out the new hire information with the Civic Center, not knowing if I could work there I called Lieutenant Cranford to ask, and she gave me a negative. I decided to go tell Mr. Sims in person that I would not be able to work for the company because it is too close to a church, park, etc. My mother told me how much money she makes and it was very saddening because I cannot help her at this moment. While at the Tower, I have to talk with one of the coordinators about what programs were available for both my sister and me. She did not know if I could be helped or not. After dropping off my Kenni to go take the T.A.B.E. test, I went to go tell him, stating that a man meet their difficulties head up, and a boy run from them hoping they disappear. I explained that I went to prison a boy came out a man and had to conduct myself accordingly. I then went back to the building and looked around. Down stairs, I saw that there was a company called Prime Payroll so I went in to just see what was going on. I ended up talking for another job, though my background came up and I had to be truthful about it, so I told everything, then it seemed to me I was pushed out the door. I then waited in the car for Kenni, yet after getting lost and driving to Lee County.

Once we got back, I went to do some yard work though it did little to ease my pain or distress. I am down right now, especially after my dad said he was too busy to send the things he said he would last week. However, I have built patience and know much [about] how to live without. My dreams, hopes and aspirations, what happen to them now. What was all that talk about me doing things to help others and not doing anything? I must stay straight; I can at least write some more people. Til Next Time

9/6/18

I woke up at about five again today and posted something on Facebook, and then I ate and stretched. It felt good to get the kinks out before the sun come up. I then wrote like five people, asked my sister for the phone to call my dad to remind him to ship the box, and then I went out to the yard. My mother showed up and asked me to till the dirt in the little field she has. It was difficult work at first but one; I got tired a little I begin to think of better ways to get the job done more efficiently. I still feel the snag of me not knowing/ or having any income. I still tried to work it off, though it was not enough work so that I can do and relax. Funny though that is what I was after, after one hour in the field. Once finished, I went to check the mail and saw that I was approved for food stamps. I then stayed sitting in the car to make some phone calls to some people. When getting back in the house, I just lay down and browsed the internet on my mother's phone. I also had to call my dad to remind him again to send the UPS tracking number so that I can track the package and probably be able to go pick it up before Monday. I slept and thought until my mother got up. I read her a few of my poems before my granddad called to talk to me. I have to cut the grass tomorrow if Harry comes with the lawn mower. Then I will offer to cut his grass as well. I just need to find something to do. I [and] Kenni go to the Department of Labor tomorrow I will go as well if I completed the yards by then. Til Next Time. Well next time came early today, while I was talking to my mother and sister, Chip called and told me how he was doing and what he could help me to do. I guaranteed him 6 months and that is what I have to give him. I also told Harry the he could do less work and teach me more of the farm. Right now I, thinking that I can so[do] both jobs. Like a one-week on and a one-week off type of thing though I never take off.

9/7/18

Well I thought this morning just to deal with the ministry, and not the time-share things. I got up in time to do my stretches and was able to write and send out the letters I wrote from the night before. I made a plan with my mother the night before. Therefore, I went out to plant the cabbage, water them then pick up the empty metal cans. Once ready to plant, I grabbed the hose and lead it out to the garden; it was tangled and once I gave it, a little pull the pipe disconnected and water begin to rush out. I had Kenni call my mother and she came out to turn off the water, then went back to sleep. I felt the need to fix what I messed up, even though I am not strong enough to pull off a properly connected PCV pipe. I then went to the store and bought supplies to fix it, though I did not know how to turn off the water completely. When my mother came about 2 hours later, she informed me that she had some of the supplies to fix the pipes. I asked why did not the job work the first time, and found out that it was because the two times did not have enough time to dry. While the pipes were drying, Lora came and talked to us and offered me a job. I also asked Lora if she could find truck for 6 thousand dollars and she stated that she would see.

9/8/18

She stated that, that much would not be needed. I fixed the pipes, well as much as I knew to do; I just know that directions are meant to be studied, especially if you do not have any experience with what is going on. I believe I did just right, and buried the pipes when I finish.

I hope that the pipes last at least a year, then we will be able to get some professional help for the fourth time the same problem occurred. My mother went to go pay a ticket to not pay the late fee, and stayed out nearly 2 hours/ once she came back, I saw she had went to the store to get things that could have waited. I also took out her and Kenni's AC so that money will not just fly out the windows…that were the end of my day. After I just went to the internet site top [to] track the things my dad sent off, and as he stated, they will be here on Monday. He called and we talked about various things that could have waited, but it is good that he wanted to speak with me. Kenni cooked. I ate, took a shower, took my mother to work and enjoyed the scenery. Once I got back to the house, I went to sleep to get ready for the long day tomorrow.

9/9/18

I got up bright and too early in the morning, around 3, I had to use the toilet so I got up and got the timer to set for an hour. I could not really get to sleep because of the ticking though I still got some rest. Once the timer went off, I reset it half way, or as much as half way that I could get it in the dark. My last time getting up, I looked at the time and it was 4:30 better than three were though. I did not want to be late so I went to the flea market with no delays. It seemed as though I was the first one there, I could not really see and could not find my way around, however, I finally did when the memory came back to me. I set up the tent and sheets on the table and was done by 6:30am, yet, Arthur still have not arrived. At about 6:40, I decided to leave and go pick up my mother. I was hoping that that memory would come back to me, and as I drove, it surely did. I was so surprised with myself and proud. When I went and was found by my mother in Wal-Mart, she stated that she did not get off til eight, I was ready to wait. However, at 7:30 she called me to the front to leave. She took the Highway, and I was surprised because I thought she was not going to test her truck in such a way.

Once we got to the Flea market she thanked me for the set up, and I told her that Arthur was not around when I made it, so I left. The flea market went well, and I have to talk to Lora's husband about the job, and he seemed cool with me my restrictions I have with my conviction. The 1000-foot rule would not have applied to me in Florida, but I am not there and must deal with the Georgia rules. I saw many temptations, and I feel like I held up to them strongly. I do feel as though they do not even see me though, the women just have their lives going on and I am but another person around. I do feel this will keep me straight though it is really that Facebook that can get me messed up, and the traveling I plan on doing. I hope that goes well.

I still have not started doing much. We left the Flea market a little early because my mother had to use the toilet. Therefore, we went to Wal-Mart, bought dog food and some oil for the change. Once we got home, mother went to sleep and I changed the oil: First, I loosened the oil filter to see if I could, then I attempted to loosen the drain plug, but that did not work because it was striped. I had to go with what I knew, so I took off the oil filter then cranked up the can a few times to let the oil drain out of the filter's hole. It was a messy job, but I got it done in the end.

I talked to Charles though he said he was going to call me back and did not. I also attempted to get with Marty, yet he did not answer the phone nor did he call me back. I then went to feed the dogs and let them out together and Tazz was close to penetrating

Diamond, so I had to lock them back up. Seeing that I was not going anywhere because, Harry had to drive to Atlanta. In addition, Marty did not call me back. I worked out a little then took a shower. Once I was done, I went to write some letters. I woke up mother at nine, and liked that she got most of her sleep caught up with. I did not want to drive so she did. I came back home at some peach cobbler. "Serve first then the money will come" I ended with that one.

I woke up at 3 then turned the timer a full circle so that I could be woken at four, then half circle, and got up at 430. I wrote a little then ate and used the toilet before leaving at around 545. I still proceeded to get to the flea market before 630 because I used the highway. I unpacked one box and put up the tent before Arthur came.

9/11/18

I did not write yesterday, and really forgot of what I did the day before or I just do not feel like writing at all, about yesterday. Today I woke up at 7:00, because I was up waiting for Gerclure to call, but she did not. I was tired but still went out to help my mother to till and fix the gate because Tazz got out the cage. While I sat fixing Diamond's cage Tazz begin to start biting the cage and pushing it with his snout

9/18/18

Wow, it has been a while since I have written, and was encouraged to start back adamantly. There has been time I just made excuses to not do this because I have been thinking ...Why?

Though I was challenged to think of the most inspiring officer I could, and nothing showed up, I just hit a blank. I know that I use[d] to appreciate some officers and not others. I remember the ones who were just too much for themselves though I do not remember the ones who made it a better place each time they worked. I won't lie, I do remember some who were very good to me maybe too good, yet to other they were just crazy. Well my point of this is just to inform people, of my conclusions when I was attempting to think back: It seemed like I've been gone for years when I attempted to look back to an experience that only took place 3 weeks ago. This is very scary to me because when I use[d] to ask people who have been down for years, like 15 plus, of what did the people they saw come and go, say of the reason they came back, I even asked a few. It was because they forgot the experience they received from prison; the brick walls, the loneliness, the orders and control of the officers who were human as themselves. It seems, now it is the same thing I experienced in a smaller scale with my looking back.

I must put a lot of emphasis on my support group, and what I'm allowed, or held back from doing now that I'm home; My mother number one, has established, or love me enough to allow me to stay with her without stressing me of anything, neither Job nor money. I help with the only resources I have though, my body and mind. She asks then I ask for what then do. Not having a television, which those who knew me inside will attest to me not being a big fan of, helps me not pacify my mind within the "box." I am able to think as much of myself then the things around me, seeing my adjustments and being able to notice the good bad and ugly. Another thing is I not having the availability to travel with my own vehicle. My mother's vehicle is available though it is hers and not being able to pay for gas and maintenance. I do not use it much. So being unwilling to travel much helps for me to stay still and observe myself. I am not saying I do not go places and do things, it's just I have time to help myself with my mental and spiritual adjustment. I am not going to keep this away because it was a big subject in prison; marriage, sex life and opposite sex relationships.

Wow this is tough to disclose, I really do not know why, well it is not, because it is important. Ok, as inmates we are deprived of intimacy with the opposite sex unless one is doing wrong, though natural thing with a staff member. I had my urges, though I fought those urges off a good bit of my time (nearly half). As a side note that is not long at all. I fought my urges off because my charge and the reason I let myself in the prison doors in the first place. Being a sexual slave, a slave to sex, was the reason I felt the need to be accepted and forced someone to have sex with me. I had the urges not only because they are natural, also because I intentionally decided to lust after females. I never got in the gunning thing, never did it though I was close at a time when an officer showed openly that she was sexually attracted to me? I even attempted to look her up on Facebook because of my delusional promises to her. Well, I "put on" as some will say. Knowing she would come walking in I got a good sweat in while I was in the cell alone, fogged the window then bent down and looked away when she passed my window. It was bait and worked. She stopped and asked what I was doing, I turned around, put my finger to my lips in a shush jester. She looked up and down and grinned from ear to ear, I only had my shirt off.

From then on, until she was fired she gave me much attention, and I was soaking it up inside, though denying it on the outside.

My point of saying this was to say we are deprived in there, though I have not been tempted out here where there are millions of females to choose from. Yes, I have flirted and have been flirted back to, though my goal is to only have sex with my future wife, though as my goals and prison had to be adjusted, these goals may have also, though about 70% of my want to love and adore a half. Though I work to love and adore most, because I feel that is the best way to live. I got a little depressed with thinking that I was just bumming around, however, I had to rethink that and reevaluate my purpose and goals. I have goals for years though I have to adjust them to tailor with my own situation and circumstances that I did not know would exist when I was in prison developing them.

I think I have memory problems because of my football days, so it is hard for me to think back and remember the specific days I am trying to write about. In addition, I might go back further than I hope to and repeat some things. This is a mishmash of the days missed in this journal. I know that social media have a lot to do with my procrastination. I have made a Facebook, integral, and LinkedIn to connect with people which connections are only superfluous. Whatever that means hahahaha.

Yesterday, I helped disassemble a Hoop (growing) house, which took most of the day. The day before that I helped fix up a fence that a person and I started about a week before. On Saturday and Sunday, I got up between 4 and 5 to head to the Flea market to sell my mother things she buy or is given for a small profit. I have worked, for the sake of doing something though nothing for much money, because I do believe I must serve first, and then the money will eventually come. I still wish that it would hurry up. I am proud that I have said some inspirational things both on social media and in my letter back to my brothers. I am tired of writing right now; I hope to grab this again before I go to sleep

9/20/18

Wow its now six twenty in the morning and I have cried. Why? I do not really know why. However, let me tell you what I have done this morning. First I woke up like 4:30am and saw that no one had connected with me on my phone, so I begin to travel my mind hoping something would come, so that I could post...I forgot the post, however I did post something inspiring. Then I went to do other things, but was drawn back to my phone and the internet. Note that I do not have any do not contact orders for my victim, if you know my mess you can probably guess why. Therefore, I must also back track to when I found out through the white pages, which I hope is legal that she got married and changed her name. I saw that she did not have a public profile on Facebook nor LinkedIn so I went to Instagram and so that her bio stated that she was a domestic violence survivor. Yes, she survived my foolishness and now it is a part of her life that I ignorantly created. My mind just went jumping to places I had visited in the past, things that I had said and promised. One thing is that I will be one who is not afraid to be alone, one who would wear my past to help other's future. I then got the idea to do this by updating my bio; I tried multiple times with no success.

Then because I could not do that, I decided to go a step further and post my past action on my social media pages. I just learned how to screenshot a couple of days okay so I went to the link I remembered and screenshot it then posted on my Facebook , with a quote of mushrooms comparisons to pain and such. I then went on Instagram and did the same. While doing that, I either imagined that I would lose friends or gain them and that reminded me of my mission statement, which hopefully is easily assessable on/in this book, if it is ever published. This had me turn my phone on silent, and think about the results of my posts. What will my mother think, and or others think. I am alone and it is silent right now. My belief is that silent and isolation is the seats of wisdom. I love the time I spend and in silence and with myself and I have confidence that it did not steer me wrong. Thinking about my promises and my phoniness if I do not do what I remember I said, made me cry. Thinking about the way I have hurt a person made me cry. Thinking about being lonely and misunderstood when it would never be so made me cry. A couple of days ago when I was riding to take my mother to work, I had the urge to cry and could not, so I asked her when was the last time she cried, and she answered, though did not ask why I asked. It is a big difference in prison; we are much more personal there. I understood/understand that she loves me and want the best for me; however, she cannot read my mind and is living her own life.

The light is finally beginning to show at 6:56 am and I can now do my daily stretch and breathing routine…. Til Next Time.

9/21/18

Well today, I woke up at 4:30am expecting someone to call though they did not. Therefore, I did my daily routine, with the stretching and thinking. Then went out to weed eat the grass my mother said she would, what am I here for if I do not catch on to her subliminal messages. Knowing she has to work and would be tired afterwards she says things, it seems just to see if I will do them or not, it got me good and tired, when it got hot a just sat and enjoyed nature.

My mother came back from shopping at around ten and I had just picked up the mail. It was from Michael Murphy and Carlos

Fountain. I loved to hear from them, and both letters were enlightening and funny. It truly is better to spread the love, and show those guys that someone care for them. I just laid down, search the internet for like 4 hours before Wayne Wilkes called, and I talked to him about the transition from prison. He did 27 years, compared to my almost seven. We encouraged each other to keep going despite the hardships. I then went out to till some of the garden, it was hard work because of the dry dirt, yet I made it through to get some of the grass. I place videos and pictures of the before garden and have to do something to it so that my word can get me some work. All in all, the day came and went…I am sore and ready to call it a day. I still be hoping I can have deep conversations with people though everyone is so busy, well not my cousin Stacy though it seem as though he see what I'm unable to in me. Oh yea I haggled with some grant people over 50 dollars. They are saying I can get 20000 dollars for 50 it is hard to believe. I attempted to bride [bribe] the representative with 10000 but he wouldn't take it, I am not wasting on a prayer, I have to take action, though first I have to be patient and can't spend what I am not making back. Til Next Time

9/23/18

Well this is my 27th day, the day I planned to stop writing; I know I missed a lot of events and feelings. That is an example to show how time can get in the way of things we want to be important. I wish that this will help others, I apologize that I did not dedicate as much time as I should have to this. Fortunately I am not done yet, I'm still not officially working, I'm doing odd and end jobs, if you all could look at me on my Facebook to see, you would see some of the yard work and low compensation jobs I've been doing. Today, I went to the flea market with my mother and made about 50 dollars that was about the same as when I worked for Wal-Mart eight years ago. It went well I said hello to probable a little more than one hundred people. I love to just communicate. I told Arthur's friend that I just got out of prison, and he seemed ok with it. He just said that he could not do any time in prison, and that is a good thing to me because he would not do anything to go, or will do anything to get out of trouble. Too many people have heard that I had gone to prison and still ask if I committed a felony or not.

Yesterday was a slow day. I went to a workshop at Home Depot and learned how to create a backsplash for the kitchen, or even do something with a kitchen. After wards, I mostly relaxed until it was cool enough to weed-eat the grass. After weed eating, I raked up the grass left behind then piled it up, messaged for a long time with a female that commented on my page about my picture. I encouraged her to get back into yoga and a proper diet, and agreed to keep her inspired as much as I could. My plan is to Spread Love in every way, at every chance I can.

9

BACK IN THE GAME

The Making of M.A.C. Logistics Transport

Being a sexual offender creates a lot of brick walls when it comes to employment. No one wants to hire a felon and surely not a registered offender. I knew the only way out of my financial hole was to be my own boss. With limited resources, I knew it would be a challenge but I had absolutely nothing to lose but everything to gain. I decided to drive trucks. The process was long and challenging, so I'm offering knowledge to those who may be in a similar situation as I was – attempting to re-enter the game of life and become a self-sufficient man. I've been told so many times to pray about my situation and that God would see me through. Reestablishing myself in society wasn't easy and I'm still working toward that, but I've made some bold moves. I had to do more than just pray about it. I had to work harder than I've ever worked. I had to come out of my comfort zone. I had to stretch myself beyond what I thought I was capable of. I've had sleepless nights and days full of doubt, but my hard work paid off.

I'm not dismissing faith, yet I've always been full of questions and have always been a wanderer with religion. Never pushed to go to church, yet always wondered. I remember in my adolescent years, my siblings and I went to church every weekend with most of the neighborhood kids. While playing sports, I listened intently to the teams' chaplains and others pray. I always wondered, why?

Working so hard in sports and never seeming to excel coupled with always becoming injured, I wrote off God. I told several teammates if God was real, he would strike me down now. Some looked at me in terror, others in awe. That off-season was my best; I was the closest to 100% than I had ever been while in college.

I remember going in for half time and probably one-third of the entire stadium was chanting my name. I felt as though nothing or anyone could stop me from reaching my goal of becoming an NFL player. I lasted only six games and was out for the season with a neck injury. During the fifth game, after assisting on a tackle I attempted to stand back up but was "struck down" by the numbness of my legs. I was moving them but couldn't feel them. Within two weeks, I lost fifteen pounds and went into a shell. I attempted to drown myself in sex and video games. I cut myself with a razor blade approximately thirty times for memory that my body let me down. I attempted to make a success out of a career in the military but my trouble with law enforcement in the past was too much for me to qualify. I graduated and attempted to start a career at Wal-Mart, though I was constantly reminded that I was a failure every time I looked at my check and calculated a s e v e n dollar an hour wage after taxes. I knew I was better than minimum wage. I knew I had the smarts and skills to excel to the high standards I set for myself. I was better than minimum wage and I refused to settle for mediocrity.

During three months of not working, I helped someone who was like a father to me; he was a great friend. He taught me how to establish relationships with truck rental companies. I set up insurance ($2,400) to activate my federal authority; MC#, without having a physical truck with the knowledge I found from Facebook. I set up accounts with all three major rental companies (Ryder, Penske, and Budget). I also learned from Facebook about dispatchers and how carriers can hire or be their own dispatcher through the load boards. Its process is from shipper to broker to a dispatcher to the carrier to driver to receiver/consignor - with many variations.

I decided to go to C.D.L school which costs $1,800. Attending school and driving back and forth from school to work plus truck rentals and planned trips added up to approximately $4,000. I inquired about many jobs with multiple companies and was denied because of my sexual battery conviction and the young age of my C.D.L. license. I established my LLC while still in trucking school. It cost $400. I went to work in the Virgin Islands and saved about $10,000 in five months. I was determined to get the funds I needed for my trucking business. Failing was not an option, yet I was almost sidelined from my entrepreneur journey by an accident that could have left me paralyzed. While in the Virgin Islands working for a company called Florida Welding doing steel fabrication and erection, attempting to please my co-workers/team, I paid less attention to the severity of what was going on. Moving from one task to the other, letting my safety rope be free enough so that it would not constrict my movements, and focusing on the task ahead were all were things that pushed my mind away from properly making sure I was safe.

While holding a panel, getting ready to move it to the scrap pile, I stepped back, and there was nothing there to hold my weight or momentum from falling through the roof. I first heard the skylight panel give way. While falling, I reached out for something to grab. What I grabbed was a sharp flimsy panel and its only job was to bend with pressure and cut me with its rigid edges. I dropped so fast that my fall could barely be observed. I remember flashes when I hit a pallet and then hit the floor. Both hits played a major part in my survival; the pallet because it slowed my fall down just enough so that my final impact wasn't as severe. The hit on the floor because it was only sixteen feet below and didn't have any dangerous debris to further puncture me.

On my final impact, I felt tingling through my whole body. My initial thought/ prayer/ wish was that I was not paralyzed.

I took a few hard breaths, ignoring the shouts after me, and made sure that I could move and feel both my fingers and toes. I rolled over in pain but was more relieved that I had some mobility. I couldn't talk immediately after rolling over to my back, but I heard the concern, so I forced my vocals to respond.

After beginning to talk, all I could think of is how I let my team down by being so careless and stupid. I expressed my disappointment in myself through tears and sobs for too many long moments. I was admitted and released from the hospital within a couple of hours with eight staples and a sore shoulder. One week after the fall and one week of thinking back and forth on whether to stay or leave the Virgin Islands, I decided to leave. While the job is still dangerous, I could have been more careful, I could take more preventative measures to protect myself and others from accidents. Unlike football, I did not have to continually run as fast as I could into humans that are twice as big and strong as me. I could have taken preventative measures to make it less likely for me to hit the floor falling through a roof from any height.

I decided to stay two more weeks and set goals that I had a better chance of reaching by staying in the Virgin Islands. My goals, my struggle, my mission - while they're risky, they are mine. My only recommendation is that you join them; let me play the game I have chosen. Support me on my journey. Upon returning to the states from the Virgin Islands, I didn't work for anyone but took some time to relax and study. During that time, I studied all I could to learn how to be my own boss. Google and Facebook became my primary instructors. I learned about hiring a factoring company from two to four percent to factor loads, which is necessary when a company first starts without immediate capital to wait for payments from shippers/brokers. Factoring companies are either non-recourse or full recourse. Non-recourse are the companies that take a risk and will not charge the carrier if the shipper does not pay their bill. Full recourse is the opposite.

Brokers are the go-between carriers and shippers to get freight moved. Shippers are between Net 15 to Net 90 which means they pay between 15 and 90 days, so the factoring company plays like a bank and front the carrier the money owed by the broker.

I contacted brokers through my apps, sent out my Carrier Packet and/ or filled out theirs, haggled a little about price, made sure that the truck can hold (size and weight) the load, received and signed then sent back rate confirmation, picked up the load, received the Bill of Laden (BOL), then signed and sent to the broker to confirm pick up. While driving, I learned to pay attention to the HOS (Hours of Service) travel time and fuel consumption. I kept a record of each time I refueled for the IFTA (International Fuel Tax Agreement) report. Once the Load is dropped, the BOL must again be signed; then sent to the broker for confirmation. To get paid, I send an invoice to my factoring company. This invoice includes an account assigned form showing a summary of the following pages, which is a rate confirmation and a signed BOL for each load I want to be factored in that specific invoice.

Below is a breakdown of my expenses for the first week I was out by myself as the dispatcher, carrier, driver, and office clerk.

On a 500 mile per 6-day per week

A constant and necessity = Insurance. Averages out to $2,600 per month/ $650 per week/ $108per day/ .21 per mile

Rental. $ 2400 per month/ $600 per week/ $90 per day/.18 per mile

Rental .20p/m mileage on a 3000 mile per week scale.$2,400 per month/ $600 per week

Fuel on a 3000-mile week $4200 per month/$1050 per week

Subscriptions also run about $300-$600

For just expenses above is $12,000 per month /$3,000 per week/ $1 per mile

To add a semi with my sister as the driver without a trailer is twenty thousand yearly,$7,200 for the first month then $4,990 monthly after.

An apportioned registration plate will cost about $2000 per year (it is just a license plate to go through multiple states) IFTA stickers will also be needed to register burned fuel in every state for about $6.

On the verge of just taking more time to get out on the road, I reached out to a Facebook trucker group, detailing my financing and concerns. Many people reached out, telling me I should just wait and build more capital. One guy reached out and gave me inspiration and a wealth of knowledge. He even dispatched me for a week to make some money while I waited for my MC# to become active. I only made enough money to pay for the rental, so I was desperate and took his offer to drive with him for a week, then drive his truck to build some capital. After driving/riding for a week, I soaked up all the knowledge I could, and it was great I did because he did not pay me the agreed amount of money. Money is not the main objective; it is the first comfort, then happiness and lastly, money.

To purchase and own my own truck would be great. My main concern is breakdowns and repair costs. With a rental truck, repairs are part of the bill. The only way I will feel comfortable getting a truck is to have a company to contract with to have them on call if anything goes wrong mechanically. It's some great money in trucking, but the main reason I feel they go out of business is the paperwork. One can start knowing and doing basically nothing, but when that audit comes around, they begin scrambling, not making money then go under. This is just my theory.

I recall a few days of my journal when I wrote affirmations in my journal which helped me push forward towards my goals and to be a better me.

9/23/19

"We have to know more than what we understand"

I think no matter how old one becomes the quote, "if I only knew back then, what I know now."

Sacrifice my present for my future; Sacrifice today for tomorrow; Yes, live for the day but when tomorrow comes, you better be ready.

It may seem like I knew I was sacrificing today for tomorrow, by running headfirst into people in hopes to get millions. Though really, I was releasing my pains, forgetting my struggles, and attempting to make people proud and trust me those days.

Don't allow your struggles today to hinder your progress tomorrow. Positions don't change people; people adjust based on positions. Find out a person's habits, you then find that person.

Our habits define us.

We must heal ourselves as dependents before we can heal as independents.

As with people, places, and things (nouns)—we treat that what's new (interested strangers), with admiration, awe, tenderness, care, concern, and/or respect. The old gets thrown around and dirtied as though it will always be there. Keep your shoes, family, houses, friends, cars, and clothes clean and respected, then their 'travel time will reach astronomical levels.

The above quote was inspired many years ago, though it comes to mind constantly, I was reminded just this morning (9/20/2019). I was placing my "New" laptop in my "New" laptop bag and took extra time to find the soft cushion which protects my screen. I wondered how long this treatment will last. Then, I thought ahead and realized, not long, because when my screen becomes scratched and or the outside becomes dirty (common), I will begin devaluing the looks.

 This is my reason for writing this book. I believe authors write books based on what they wish they had available for themselves. I begin to believe that we are created and connected to a knowledge that we will never comprehend, a knowledge that will always appear in times when we need it though, so many wish not to accept that knowledge, cover it up with mind-altering substances, and or distractions.

"Social Media should not be our connection with the world, yet a Tool to connect with the world".

I thought of this quote while on detox from food and my phone– the outside world. I was thinking of turning on my phone 24 to 34 hours earlier than I had planned, because; it doesn't make me, I don't have to do this, were all the things that went through my mind.

But to connect with people, to see how they are doing, I would have to go to social media. And why when there is a much bigger world outside of social media that I have not explored. Would I allow myself to be chained to social media, allowing it to be my only means of networking, socializing, and communicating? No, I will not. I realize that it is one of many tools to connect, but it is not my connection, period.

12/28/19

There comes a time when one must realize that they have been living wrong and need to change, slow down, speed up or just stop and evaluate what is really going on. I accept that some people are just not willing to accept the life lessons of others, sometimes, not even themselves. I have also come to realize that I am not one of those people that will accept being unhappy for too long. I am not one of those people that can just suck up the things I think are wrong with another person and hold it in, just to not cause problems within our connection. I am a person that believes in the possibilities which have been given us all–unlimited possibilities. I believe in the day when I will be content and happy with myself, which includes my past, present, and future. I believe that I will be content with person(s) knowing me and I know them. I will, and they will be comfortable with making mistakes, learning from them then moving on to remembering the mistakes and consciously dissecting them, to try not to make those mistakes in the future.

All this comes through listening and absorbing what others around us go through and tell us. I have made many mistakes in my recent past; mistakes that had been taken lightly, but could have been futile to my survival in this world, which most call freedom. I ignored counsel from those that I will not ever be able to fathom the knowledge they have between their ears, behind their present, and in front of their eyes. Walking with a semi-sure step and on the balls of my feet to move quickly, I came to realize a couple of my shortcomings of my time on this earth, a shortcoming that can sway either to the loving or hating hearts of others.

An Open Letter to Sex Offenders

Dear Sex Offender,

My name is Maurice Harris and I am also a sex offender. My reason for writing you is to give advice on what to expect during the stages of being a registered sexual offender. These stages include the prison/jail time, after prison. Most people are shocked when they go to prison and experience the way people treat them. My advice is to change your mindset and whatever made you commit your crime or put you in the position to be blamed for your crime. If you are a sexual offender, it means you were convicted. Meaning, it is your crime to own for life. Your crime, now doing the time, is a reality that you alone have to deal with. The best way to deal with the time is to accept the crime as yours. Evaluate your situation and the way people will treat you, both good and bad people, not to exclude the understanding and the ignorant ones. I believe and understand in a way, which allows me to be humble and through my example, I try to give people explanations of why they do things. I attempt to keep my mind open in a way that judges with most facts, and I ask you to do the same.

You must judge yourself as others will judge you, e.g., how will a murderous, neglected brutally raped when a child, drug dealing predator, judge you? He would probably try to blame you or your kind for his problems, or the reason he is now in prison for the rest of his life. How would you respond when meeting this person? My suggestion is to first change or open your mind. Our minds were closed when we allowed ourselves to be consumed by a situation that placed us in a point of life where we can meet someone so sinister. Your mind must be set and open to both the good and bad that will come with being a sex offender.

Once you get out, you must think of how society and/ or the officers will treat you when you go to register. One of the common sayings that I believe is valid more times than not is "first impressions." People treat others based on the first time they meet them. I have been registered in two states and the Virgin Islands and all of the officers acts as though they respect me. It may be because they are respectful people or it can be because of how I conducted myself in the first meeting and on. It is conservative, but still relevant in this world, the small "yes/no ma'am/sir", "excuse me", and apologies. The little things make a difference and are very meaningful to people even if they seem to act opposite.

Maurice Harris

My Call To Action

THERE IS WAY TOO MUCH free time in jail to sit and think. Too often the thoughts can be negative and damaging to one's mind and future - it was for me. Instead of falling into the trap of beating myself up, I chose to find a way to benefit from all my free time. I had a thirst for knowledge of myself and my future while incarcerated. I needed the tools for success that were unavailable to me, so I decided to create my own plan. One would probably wonder how someone sitting behind bars, waiting for a prison sentence could have the mind to create anything.

Well, believe it or not, not everyone sitting behind bars is a no-good menace to society. Many inmates have college degrees, families, and obviously made some bad choices and are meeting the consequences of their actions. I was one of those college degree men, and there I was sitting behind bars with an active mind wanting to create and build.

The isolation and idle time in jail allows the mind to be clearer, thoughts are purer and creativity (if allowed) surfaces in the most unusual ways. I absorbed information from other inmates and used their thinking patterns to formulate a plan to help others who may be searching for those tools for success as I was. Self-inventory is crucial to success.

There were several questions that came to mind that I should have had the answers to before I ended up in a jail cell awaiting sentencing. Why didn't I have the answers? I had no guidance!

Besides my mother, no one was truly concerned about my future unless it was related to football. I made up my mind to get my life together. Growing up in a single-family household, I fought the odds and was fortunate enough to attend Florida State University. While there, I participated in and was the guest speaker for various community service events. I was honored to win the Atlantic Coast Conference (ACC) Community Service Hour Award. This award was for having the most community service hours of FSU football players. I encouraged young children to pursue their education and to stay out of trouble. Little did I know, I'd soon need a taste of my own medicine.

Nevertheless, in December of 2011 while sitting in my jail cell, P.L.E.A. C.A.S.E was birthed. P.L.E.A. C.A.S.E: **P**ersonal **L**egal **E**ducational **A**thletic **C**omprehension **A**dvice **S**upport **E**ncouragement.

PLEA CASE

The mission of PLEA CASE is to reach out to any and all, who are willing to reach inside themselves to *identify* unique capabilities, *produce* self-esteem, and *develop* flexibility and adaptability for effective behavior in an ever-changing world. Pleading the case is the first step of the program to allow the participants to actually plea to themselves, their case, and choose if their past life is defined as being innocent, guilty, no contest, or neutral. I befriended inmates from a variety of backgrounds who allowed me to interview them as participants of PLEA CASE. I questioned the inmates about their tendencies, reactions, and mindsets before, during, and after their detrimental actions that led them to prison. While learning about them, I was learning about myself. I advised and counseled inmates of all ages and social backgrounds.

A set of specific questions is given to the participant to complete to allow me to become familiar with them and empathize with their past episodes, present circumstances, and future goals. I wished I had someone to do this with me before incarceration. Sometimes, a roadmap is all one needs for a little direction. After the questionnaire, a skeleton interview, tested and proven, to delve into the psychological triggers is conducted. The interview is the foundation of the growth process.

I'm speaking from experience when I share with participants of how one wrong decision, no matter how small, can change one's life. I am living proof that regardless of the circumstances, you can be successful in every aspect of life. I took the ASVAB and received multiple reference letters from the Army. I had accumulated eight charges since middle school and wasn't sure I'd be accepted in any branch of the military. I took the test and received a decent score – enough to choose several jobs I'd be interested in. I graduated from high school in August of 2010 and was disqualified from the Army in October of 2010 because of the excessive amount of charges I had.

I also worked at Wal-Mart as a temp employee thinking I would become a department manager after six months because of my college degree. After an entire year and several interviews, I still wasn't selected for a better position and only made about seven dollars an hour after taxes. There was no goal and no direction in my life. I was living day to day with no purpose. I believe we are built for what life gives us. I've overcome many obstacles and challenges in life and I've only begun to scratch the surface of my purpose, my dreams.

The educational aspect of PLEA CASE is most important as life is always a learning experience. Whether in the classroom, workplace, home, or even walking in the park, there is something to learn. I learned a lot on the fields and in the classrooms of FSU and also behind bars. I was open-minded enough to recognize and receive whatever lesson life was teaching me at the moment and that is the key – being open-minded.

Reaching back to help others is important for the building of relationships and the community. It then reaches outside of the community and eventually, cities, states, and ultimately the nation will benefit. Healthy relationships are one controlling factor of cognitive thinking. Having others who truly care praising your positives and admonishing your negatives helps build self-esteem and confidence. It also allows one to be a progressive product of society. Nothing is accomplished alone and to know the tendencies of yourself is to know the possibilities of the human race.

Here is when my perspective about me changed. This is my journal entry while in prison:

1/2/20

I changed my mind and accepted my decision coupled with the results of me being a sex offender by taking myself and my feelings out of the situation. I took my feelings of who I am as a person and who I wish to become out of the incident and placed a stranger as the perpetrator and an innocent loved one as the victim. How will I feel then? Would I want them to walk free as I use to think I should, or would I want them to do time and learn from their bad decision? I chose the second one because I did my time and came out a better person because of it. I know that it is based on the person and circumstances, this method came about because I saw the most miserable and happy people in prison, and I needed to be one of the happy ones.

JOURNALING BEYOND BARS
Part 2

Journaling was such an important escape for me while I was serving time. It was also one that I continued after my release. You have already read the first 27 days; these are my journal entries beginning with Day 28 through Day 63. *(As previously stated, these are unedited and personal documented pages from my personal journal that I kept. (For the purpose of publishing, punctuation and missing words may have been added to be more readable.) It may sound like I'm rambling and some may make no sense at all, but these were my personal thoughts and never meant to be publicly shared.)*

9/24/18

Yesterday, I ended my day with helping someone ship two goats from someone else's house to his own. We threw them across the fence to a place where they would be temporarily. Then once we made it back to my mother's house, right before dark, we put fertilizer on the greens to hopefully help with their growth. I was offered money, though refused it, even though I am short on money, I believe the learning experience, service and bond is more beneficial than any amount of money at this point. I had him dedicate to his mission to get things done.

This morning I woke up later than I thought I would, six. I got up posted some inspirational things on Facebook, then went about my daily routine. After watering the greens, I pulled some of the grass that was too close for comfort. Then, I decided to weed eat a section of the yard that had too much covering around a stomp. The person came as he said he would around 9:45am, then we headed to his house to finish the goat fence. It was a little before two when we finished transferring the two females to the area that needs eating down. We then went out to eat some Chinese food and stopped for the day. When getting back to my mother's house I sat down and relaxed outside and sitting there for almost 3 hours napping.

During my sit, I thought about how I am on fire for serving and helping people. I try to make as many inspirational quotes I can for those who follow me. However, I wonder if it is worth it, if anyone really benefiting from it. My mind is set no matter the response I get, I must keep spreading love.

9/25/18

Today was an interesting one. I have to begin at before I went to sleep. I asked my mother what was on the agenda for the next day, and she told me to put the 7dust on the greens, with a stocking for an even coat. I wrote it down then lay down. I got up at a little before
six, did my stretching routine and ate some oatmeal and peanut butter for the second day in a row to get me started. Soon as it was light enough to go out I told her my intentions, yet she told me she

had not found a stocking to use for the dust. I heard her and thought that she was not going to find it so while she looked I improvised. She did not like my improvisation, so hurried out with a stocking. I then placed the dust on the plants, cleaned my hands and gloves, and then got ready to head out to run errands and wash clothes. While out, I first went out to get a study guide for the motorcycle test then went to make a deposit in my checking account. While on the way to the bank, Kenni called me stating she had to be in a lawyer's office in 20 minutes. I went and made the deposit then headed back home.

Once home, Kenni was not ready, and I said something about it. Was also at the house ready to leave, and told me that we had something to do later on in the day; I was excited for that. During the time I had alone in the house, I studied the motorcycle book, listened to, and watched videos on 7dust and pesticides. My mother and Harry came back early and made plans for us to do something; I just really had washing my clothes and the motorcycle test on my mind. Once Kennithia came back, I waited a few, making sure no one had to do anything, then headed towards the laundry mat. After only a couple of minutes in someone spoke to me, and stated that he recognized me, he had to explain several details of our dealings 13 years ago for me to just vaguely remember him.

9/26/18

I left off there because I had to go to sleep. I attempt to lay down no later than 11 because it seems as though I cannot help but to wake up early. So I will continue where I left off yesterday. I remembered him, in a way I remembered his brother and father, because he was an under classman at the time. However, I felt an opportunity to share my story and that I did. He stated that he could connect me with someone who may be able to arrange a speaking engagement, I was happy to hear. Then he invited me over to meet his father, knowing that his dad would like to see me. Once we got to the restaurant that his father owned, I recognized him as soon as I seen him though I did not remember his name. I sat by him and told him where I have been all these years and he asked what for. I told him, and he was surprised at how long I did in prison, and thinks that mostly every man has done the crime. I hope that it is not true for the sake of this world. Quay his son was correct in saying that he knew people, because in a few minutes I was on the phone with a lieutenant of police telling my story and hopefully getting a speaking engagement at the University here.

That was amazing how fast that worked. While talking I was asked what I do for work, and told that I farm here and there, with that they stated that they may have a need for greens because their connect just went out and they may have room to hire someone else. I exchanged contact info and went about my way once the restaurant closed. Once I got my clothes, I went off to the D.M.V. to take a test to get my permit to ride motorcycles. I passed with a 90 missing two questions I do not even remember reading about in the study book. Afterwards I did not do much, really just explain what happened during the day and went to sleep.

Today I woke up at about 4 40 and wish that I had not, but it worked out because I needed some time to get my mind right and come up with a game plan. I posted an inspirational quote, and then started my morning with some oatmeal and peanut butter. I then went through my routine. I did not have anything to do so I just waited until light, went, and gave the greens some attention, taking a picture of them and sending them to my dad. My mother had to leave and take care some business, so I was mostly stuck, yet I would not have asked to use the truck because I do not have the money to do anything. I begin typing and creating a bio for the ministry when Lora called and asked would I help her move something in her storage. I gladly accepted, she came an hour later after I thought she had lost her way or changed her mind. We left, and I forgot both my water bottle and lunch, though I knew that it would be an ok. I just did not want to spend unnecessary money to buy food when there is some at the house. The storage was a job and we did not finish before she had to leave to go pay some bills, though we made much progress. I [r]an out to go and wake up my mother to go to work then take a shower for bed. Til next time

9/27/18

Well its 8o clock and I have been up a little over 2 hours and had to pull myself out of the bed for some reason. First, because it was so close to six, I have to think of something to write to my one unofficial client and social media. I also decided to text some people good morning. Well I decided to write in this journal because of a feeling that came over me, I would first start from the top. I hope that I have not written most of this, I do not know because I rarely read back, the editor will get it though.

Ok I may have said that I have been trying to network on multiple social media sites: Facebook, Instagram (because of Anna Maria), and LinkedIn (because of my victim). These are two people from my past Anna Maria is from 10th grade, I talked to her a little before I changed my number on house arrest. I found them both on the white pages, trying to see how they were doing. Anna, I texted (she had the same number since 10th grade),"victim" I attempted to text. Anna encouraged me to get a Instagram after She explained why she doesn't have a Facebook. I was texting strong, trying to encourage her because I saw much pain within her post and she also explained to me she do not trust anyone. I was attempting to spread love and adoration, though she finally told me in not so blunt words to back off, because of her life is busy and really do not include me. I did not attempt to contact "victim" besides the text for a couple of days. However during my networking, I begin to follow a radio host, and asked was she able to get me on her show to inform people about my past bad decisions and their potential to make the same ones. After writing she would try to pitch it, a few days later she explained to me that she did not want to open any old wounds with the victim. Therefore, I took it upon myself to contact the victim, hoping that "victim" will consent and assist on this amazing journey.

Now, I get to my morning occurrences, it was only finding out that "victim" has blocked me on both Instagram and LinkedIn. It was hurting, thinking about how we ended our relationship. That was even selfish for me to say, because I just stopped writing her, I did not even read the last letter she wrote to me, 22-year-old selfishness. Now that I have grown and forgave, I expect "victim(s)" to do the same thing. Yes, I have multiple victims when I truly think about it; Anna Maria is one of them. Most who were exposed to me were "victim," trust this is not easy to write in this journey even with only me reading, not knowing if any other person will ever get the chance to read this. They were victims to my ignorance and cruelty, I have two hundred plus friends on Facebook and 99% of them requested me, and I ask why, now.

Seeing such a terrible person, I was to forget, to put them on the back burner to pursue something that will never last... the only thing that last and which should be our most prized procession is our love for one another. I wish to share this love with all I am able though, my mind keeps telling me it is not possible. I do not wish, and I believe I did not wish to hurt anyone, the difference from then and now is my understanding and consideration of other's upbringing and experience. I must consider that when I think I can jump out of prison and attempt to be friends with people I have hurt in so many ways. They have grew up and left their [past] and started families are probably in the safest place they know to be. In addition, here I come trying to bring back something they have fought so hard to get away from. Though let me say I do love, and I cannot hide and love at the same time, I will use as much discretion I am taught, and feel I must have though this story must be told.

9/28/18

Well today went well. I was told last night that I would be picked up earlier than I did, however we got the things moved in only about an hour. Then, even though she knows that she is trying to watch her diet, she still went to Burger King. I did not say much to that point. The exciting part was seeing how she treated her nieces; I try to not judge because I do not know the first thing about raising kids the correct way. When I made it back, I just took a two-to-three-hour nap without even going inside. I went to check the mail and saw Candy Publishing's package waiting on me with a few letters from people I had written. They made me happy knowing that I am touching others. I did some things outside then came in to eat and read. While reading "Interactive Q&A," there was an assignment to write my thoughts so, this is why I grabbed the computer. O yea I grabbed a tripod from the storage, and now can hopefully make some inspirational videos. I will end on that and try to continue reading this book without stopping for a few. I have to take my mother to work so that we can get to the flea market in the morning, hoping for a few dollars. Til Next Time

9/30/18

The day started early yesterday, with me getting up early, about 5 oclock then getting breakfast and fixing lunch. I left around six and made it to the flea market about 15 minutes before the sun showed light enough to see. Arthur was talking of things I knew nothing about, however I answered and had a conversation as if I knew what was going on. Soon after setting up most of the items on the table, people came to get the shoes I advised my mother to bring. I did not have the patience to haggle about prices when I felt as though the shoes needed to be sold anyway.

There was also a woman who came and attempted to make me a deal on movies though she wanted them for about fifty cent apiece, and I was close to giving them to her, but she did not really want them. I had made about 25 dollars before I even went to pick up my mother because of shoes. Once I went to pick her up, me kind of set back and just greeted people as they walked by.

The flea market is a good place just to make connections, and I feel as though once I get me a vehicle, I would be able to service people and build a clientele. Dellaina called while we were at the flea market to see if Kenni was going to cook because Uncle Boo, his crew and her crew were coming. I was happy to hear that and was looking forward to their visit. I attempted to persuade Harry to do some work though he was not with it. Therefore, I just went home and chilled with the dogs until Dellaina, and Boo pulled up in the driveway about 2 hours later. It was nice to see everyone, and Boo and I had a great talk once everything calmed down. My mother was tired from working all night, though she attempted as much as she could to be a great hostess. I did as well, though I feel that I am distant at times, because I feel as though some conversations are not worth having and it is hard to stay around during them. I do want to show the Love everyone deserves though I am coming to understand that people are going to do and talk of things they want. I was tired, and knew I had to go to sleep if I wanted to be anything in the morning at the flea market.

Fortunately, my mother told me before she went to work that she would not be going to the flea market on Sunday to spend time with her brother. I know that she was going to be tired at work and when she got home though I also knew that she is more use[d] to crazy schedules than I am, I still had to go to sleep because Boo car was acting up and we had a plan to get it fixed so that he could leave as soon as possible the next day. I called Harry asking if he would help and he agreed with no hesitation. We all planned to rise early so that the alternator could be off the car and at the store when it opened at eight. I went to sleep after giving some unnecessary time to social media.

I woke up at seven on the dot, 2 hours after I had thought I would. I was glad because I knew I needed some sleep. I went to wash my face and brush my teeth then out the door to wait for Harry. Boo got up and out first, two hours later, then we got started getting the alternator off before Harry came. He did not come by the time we were stuck, nor did he answer his phone, so we went to Advanced Auto to get the alternator and tools to take it off. By the time we got the old alternator off and the new one on, Harry showed up. He stated that he had trouble with his goats and had to handle that, yet he still come with all intentions to help. Everything went well, we ate breakfast, and then I went to try to get my skate wheels off. Again I attempted to get Harry to do something, though he would not...ll I can do is ask though so I just said whatever; tomorrow should be a busy day. I had to suggest we take some family pictures; at least I am sticking with creating memories. I know that instead of just being able to talk about, when we got together, we can see when we got together. The tripod I got was much help with taking the picture, a great investment indeed. Everyone had to leave after the picture, and I truly enjoyed the time my family came and spent with us, it is treasured dearly in my head. If I can help it, I will be at every get together. Til Next Time

10/1/18

Woke up at 5:30am and had to think of things to place on social media. Once that was done, I made my way out side to feed the dogs and let them roam a little. My mother came out, so I asked what she have planned, she stated to water and hoe the greens. She eventually watered the greens, yet things came up before she has to hoe them. Therefore, I went and messed with the baby potatoes that are growing, and I did not know it. Once I got tired of that, I went to make my first video to post on YouTube. It went terrible, my phone timed out of a minute or so...so, I had to make segments, which were jumbled up once I posted them. I still posted the crappy videos because I wish people to see my progress with technology and social media period. I took a few more pictures and videos before I came and begin to read. Once reading, I saw questions that I truly need to answer dealing with my book.

In addition, I thought about my reactions to the things I have a problem with my mom's actions. I asked myself the question would I do that with someone I am trying to get to know and be with for the rest of my life. I tell my mother things that she needs to work on based on the things she tell me she want to work on, or things that affects me personally. These are expressed and known because we are stuck with each other; there is no breaking up with us. However, with a mate she as well as I will try to be on our best behavior, until we get comfortable with each other and/or have invested so much time in the relationship that we will not want it to go to waste. That is the reason one gets married, and make the vow, "Til death do us part," it suppose[d] to be a loving mother and child bond. That cannot lose its connection through trivial human tendencies.

10/3/18

The thing I have noticed about journal is that it is easy to forget if it is not on a daily schedule. I miss days not knowing it until I get back on the computer.

Yesterday was a day of waiting, I was hoping that a person called and/or came and picked me up so that I would get to work on the greens and chicken house. Though that call never came, he did not even answer his phone for me. However, I did spend some time

with my mother, hoeing out the garden. I received a priority letter in the mail, and it had a check within it, after an inspection by me and my mother, we decided that I should try it and attempt to cash it. After riding around for way to[o] long, I finally made it to a check-cashing place that would look at a cashier's check. She stated that she would not cash it even if a bank confirms there was money within the bank, because the check was fake. I thought quick, ripped the check up moments later, then texted, and emailed the results to the people on the documents that came. That was terrible, and I had good intentions to do as the instructions stated. OH Yea and I received a text from Ms. Shirley asking me to call in reference to her son, Derrick. When I called, she had told me that he was now connected on Jpay and wished for me to connect, so I did and soon after he wrote me giving me a little update. I also put several others on my account so when I do get some funds I can write them all. I received a job in the morning so I went to lie down early, so that I would be rested in the morning.

This morning I woke up at about 530 thirty minutes before my alarm was set. I took my pills, ate, then went to wake up my mother with noise from me brushing my teeth. She was already awake complaining that my cousin called her early, around three to tell her something, because he thought she was at work on lunch break. We made it to McDonalds early and just sat and talked a little. I messaged my cousin who worked at a car dealership, in hope that he could help us finance a vehicle. I forgot about this cousin until it became time he may be able to help me, sad but true.

10/4/18

Today went well. I woke up earlier and I had a job so I dropped my mom off to work so I had to car. I went to Waffle House to eat with Marty. I ordered more than he and he finished before me this time, so he had to wait for me to eat my Waffle. We then went to the job site and we cleaned up, it was a long day but it was a good. At 12, Marty had to leave, though I stayed, I couldn't work anymore after 2 because I was tired. No lunch, so it was hard on me but we got the bulk of it done. I posted pictures of before and after on Facebook from the pool. I was able to collect a tarp that was about to be thrown away, my mother and I can use it for a flooring. The canopy my mom wanted to put out in the back to hold her stuff to sell for the flea market will be great for it. I also had Marty's tools, so she has to take them to him. I received an inquiry from a guy that lived near about the job we was doing. He stated his work was a similar job, though I was unsure about the estimate, so I asked Marty to go over there with me. He didn't want to but he did and gave the guy a $450 estimate. I believe that I can do it cheaper, but the guy may not call. I then went to go wash my clothes and drop off some mail for my mom. I talked to my cousin Lil Ron telling him I may be going to Atlanta tomorrow to get the car. Hopefully my brother is okay with that's about it for today. I'm tired. I received two letters from Derrick, Black and A.J. both gave me contact info on family and friends to begin connecting. Most of them had written back and it's going good now. Til next time

Well this is October 7th and I'm at the flea market but I'm trying to catch up right now with my journals. Am catching with most of which I missed with my brother yesterday from the morning at 7 and we went here, there and everywhere in Albany. He had to go see Tora and I had to go see Harry because he had greens that my mom wanted to plant. Harry had his own greens that he wanted planted and my brother asked him if he wanted us to help. I wasn't planning on helping though we did. I wanted to go and plant the greens at my mother's house so that we could head out, but my brother didn't count and probably 3-4 hours it took for us to head out towards Atlanta making it around 2, when we supposed to [have] left at 11. We were 3 hours behind and hit five o'clock traffic, which was stressful for my brother and me, but I tried to stay as positive as possible. I got to go meet Mimi, his girl that was okay…she had about three kids and with her, so she was doing okay. She also had a boot on her foot from multiple surgeries so she did not get up. Then I left because I was planning on going to see my auntie Shalene for a long time. However I went first to go see Gaddy, thinking that he was closer and he was but it took me about

20 minutes to get to his house. He told me later that it was supposed to have taken about 5 minutes. It was his mom's birthday and she was so happy to see me, he made sure that he stated that her smile was the biggest smile that he saw in a long time because she sick. It was great. I ate food, ice cream and cake. We hung out, took pictures and I met some great people. I left there probably at 10, he had to work in the morning and I had to go to the Flea Market so it was real tough driving. Because I said I was going to my auntie Shalene house I did around 11:30. There I saw Uncle Tommy, we talked a little bit about my experience in prison and what's my goals from when I came out. It was good to see auntie Shalene, I couldn't see Torrance because he was sleeping. Then I headed out and made it to Wal-Mart around 2, dropped off the car got the truck so that I could go to the flea market in the morning. I went to sleep at around 2:30 and I woke up at about 5:36, it was terrible because I was tired at the flea market. I pulled out stuff as people bought things, which wasn't much, though it went okay. The whole day I sold and my mom pots were the only things that really [sold]. I sold them for a cheaper price than what she wanted and she lost money. I liked that we made a lot of money all together yet it was a loss for my mother. Harry came through and I tried to ask him for work with him but he said no... is there an okay day at the flea market...came back home and I slept outside for about 2 hours until my mother came...she didn't get my text to get the oil so what can I do...couldn't do anything; also she went to sleep then I went to transfer some of the

stuff from the shed to Under The Canopy that's about it for the day. I was tired so I went to sleep at about 10; set my alarm at 6; set up at 6 so I got 8 hours of sleep until next time

I woke up rested at 6 but I knew I was going to be later and then [than] I usually be am…I fix the sandwiches, fix some oatmeal, then I brush my teeth; then I was ready to go. I got to the flea market at about 645 by 30 by 20 minutes before the sun came up and Arthur who's there and he like usual but he was planning on leaving early 2 hours and my mother wasn't there and I haven't sold anything but it still was a good thing. I spoke to many people with so many people…we had good conversations... harry came. I talked to him a little bit but he disappeared before I can ask him to work on my mom…left early…we may probably $10 after making payments for the table and that was about it. I stayed until 3 because little Ron said he might come but he didn't because he said he had to pay bills on a Sunday; he was excited that he didn't have to go to work though…well I called Harry and he said that he had a job to do so I went and met him at his house, parked then got on the phone. I thought I was there for a long time but I was only there for 5 minutes before he walked up…so we hooked up the tractor and ready to go.

There was work for me to do though as time went on he just drove the tractor, talk to the client and she had hired me on to weed eat her grass and cut down trees that I was happy to get because I really didn't have anything to do the next day; so we was out there moving things that he bush hog a lot of her yard for probably until 7– until we can see anymore; then we plan to finish everything the next day…black girl…I gave her daughter one or both of my cards to let her know that I'm probable to help in any way; she could or I can and I found out that she had 14 year old child, a husband who may not wish to have another child…she said she would have one either way it go…did Owen that that was funny only left around I got home at around dirty…mom still asleep. I ate some food, showered and went to bed around 9:30

I woke up…is there any night still…I got some great sleep…woke up for the last time at about 5:30. I had to wait [wake] Harry up more call him at 6:30. I woke my mom up–not really– she was up but we talked about multiple subjects, let's go do what she needed to do and she told me that I needed to stop telling her what she needed to do. I agree so I'm at 6:30 call Harris [Harry] several times…he didn't pick up until I'm about I called the client and she was ready to go at 8:30 cuz he had to do some things so I got over at 8:30 it's just me and her and…I just me and her and we waited for Harry…or not 45 minutes…he came yet, the bear battery powered saw and weed eater he had a lot to Bush Hog not more than yesterday though… and I got some weed eating done and hopefully we can use the saw soon so I can get all of the other things done then I'm back… said he was going to come again not sure if you would but I probably will be here hoeing right now… I'm tired, so I'm going to go and eat; it is 12:51 and I am off

10/10/18

to a phone call I woke up; my dad was calling to see how I was and it really helped because take it up once up I started getting ready because we have to clean out the carport because of the storm; it was expected to be here, leave around midday…once the sun came out, I went to take the dogs out, feed them and straighten the carport. I love to this is my mom…the rain begin turn around 4…we stayed out just to see Mother Nature and we came. Around 7…and I took videos…they were cool through Phase 1 2 and 3…I want came back to the house and 8 some food…the lights went out while I was on the phone with the loan company; yes, I have to change the people that I'm with now because the work they're doing I can do myself and Save several dollars ($700); also I am going to cancel Lexington Law because what they're doing I can do is well sending out letters to the people I owe money to..well it seems like hurricane Michael hurt Panama City the most, Milton and I believe Albany only got rain…now fat 51 and I have an hour before the sun will start to show and I could go outside to see what the storm did; it's about it… until next time

How to check the transmission…you have to drive and see how the gears…then also put on the break then, press the gas; if the transmission fights against the brake or does it just stay…also check

177

AJC Atlanta something and they have sales for the Atlanta I'm just check that I don't know where I stopped that but back here I'm now at the Kingdom Hall waiting for the meat family and it be here in about 2 hours. I just didn't want to go home and come back so I say I might as well stay here hopefully they come early at about 637 so I so I able to wait waiting for 1 hour instead of 2 hours and 30 minutes like I said guys is yes I am getting overwhelmed so much trivial things; trivial like just waking up in I have to clean the yard, take out the dogs, clean their poop without getting really paid for not getting any money to help my mom pay for bills; yes, it's getting disturbing time...flash been out now so 8950 days now manage it's slow I have to tell black to slow down...the same situation as I am but he's locked up in prison, I'm free. The significance of the struggles that will come getting out of prison the things that I had to deal with or have to deal with you know what the money situation...you know what bills...no worries...send Insurance...things like that...connecting with people just staying connected with people— man that's a job in itself and then when people do not connect back, deny your request...you know to just encourage them; it's hard sometimes; it's difficult when also you have people close to better and you want better things for but they're not really trying to it's not you just fighting against they feel like they ben you've been in prison so what do you know about what's going on now and relationships you know it's crazy but there's one again.

I start then stop. I start. I don't know where I'll be leaving off; then a stop…what size start back I don't want to read back what time so today was a good day started off at 5 I woke up then 8; dresses…cut some trees down; watered the greens this is why I just can't do this thing don't work good as

10/16/18

I have just decided to write on this computer that I am at in the library. Wow the storm I let put me back, I have a bad memory and really can't or would just not l ₁₉₅ go back and write what I missed. The power is still off after about 5 days. I think the power shut off on Wednesday afternoon. Which was the 10th and I still didn't write a couple of days before that. Talk about neglect. I will start today and maybe work my way back.

Today I woke up rested and ready to get something done. I had to call my caseworker for the SNAP program to continue to get food stamps because I do not have any income as of right now. Also, I received a letter in the mail about my loan and have to fill out the proper paperwork to try to get some of my loans discharged because the school has closed.

I thought I have written more than this though I guess I have been distracted trying to get things in order to my mind, relationships to my body.

10/29/18

Even now I got distracted trying to figure out what I left on my phone and where did it go in this journal. I was told that I am a better writer than speaker, though I am a better listener and responder than anything.

My days have been flying and seem like weeks by themselves, I had been wanting to sit down and write and kind of stop my, or postpone my entries until I get them all copied down at 60 days out. I have been out now for 63 days, or as the calculator shows the 27th of august was 63 days ago. I feel my stopping point was 2 days ago when I stayed up till 3 o'clock having to wake up and go to work at six (my work is odd jobs not official). I was up because earlier that day I found a phone, from who and what kind I will not say, just that it was not stolen. And I connected to the internet I had set up and went to the internet browser and there was a porn site that popped up. And that opened a whole flood gate. All I was thinking is that, this is not my phone who will find out, it's ok to just look, and I may find someone I can talk to and probably change to get in a relationship with, she will have a past, I will have a past, though we will grow together. And thrive. Tuff thinking, I know... though, I have decided to put it all out there. As I said before though only have really decided to after the conversation I had with MS Williams, that I will really show the weak mind that invades my thinking sometimes.

I have to go and get ready now, trust I will be back to write. I suppose to be picking up the truck today if nothing happens. Well, I made it back here at about 620 and watered the greens, feed the dogs, checked the mail, ate, and took a good shower. It's now 8:34, twelve hours after Kenni, her babies and I left the house and was headed towards the destination. Kenni and Amari went inside for Kenni's class then Harmone' and I stayed out the door waiting for my mother to show up so that she could go to the bank and withdraw the money from the bank. We got some food, filled up the tank, then headed out. Atlanta took 3 hours to appear, I had to warn my mother beforehand, that it could very well be a blank trip if the guy did not keep his word and was not what he claim[ed] to be. I had only talked to him twice and didn't know him from Adam. I had only heard the temperament and experience that he had with the truck and the things he was willing to tell me.

Once at the bank, where we were set up to meet, I warned my mother again if there was someone to jump out and attempt to rob us let them know that we had to go to the bank and get the money. After multiple calls and needless texts, he finally pulled up, I inspected the truck as much as I knew how to and was satisfied with my limited knowledge of vehicles. I just had to go buy the word of this stranger that I liked because he did not go too far and oversell the car, only with the minor/major detail of their being a cracked windshield that must be replaced. He explained that's why he went so low with the truck, and even lower when I attempted to get 700 off the top. He only went for three. I drove him to his house and we did the things needed to transfer the sale. I stayed on my toes while in his home thinking that he was able to just kill me at his home and take the money. His pride and joy I have realized is his daughters; though and hoped that he was not the person to do anything rash. I was 48 dollars short and wished that he took the money like it was though he stated that we had made an agreement and I had to stick to it, and I did. My mother asked me multiple questions that I hoped she knew I knew the answer to but didn't. I had to correct her, or assure her multiple times before she realized that I had most of everything under control. I had in my head that I did not want to stay so I did not stay, and left as soon as everything was kosher. The truck drove lovely to Albany and I had enough gas in the tank to make it all the way. The fill-up was 54 dollars but it did me well. I'm just hoping for at least 57 thousand more miles, at least. I was thinking the whole way back that I wish that I was not swindled and that it is somehow that he got over on me, though I have not found proof yet.

Last night I had a great conversation with Lora, my mom's friend, now my friend because she took a liking to me, she's married. We received some understanding yesterday when she was at my house. My mother don't trust her because she flirted too much, I really don't care because she is not my wife though I did because she is married. However, yesterday's conversation after she came and brought my mother and me some food, cleared up a lot and I stayed out and let her talk herself mostly out because of that understanding. First that she have never cheated on her husband and know what she will lose if she ever did. I don't have to worry about us getting any closer than what we are because of my goals and her commitment to her husband. I just hope her husband know that or get to know me to understand my story to know that I will never attempt nor pursue a married women again.

I did not work that day and received 8 hours of sleep that morning so I was rested some. I did not do much of anything. I really don't even remember what I did. Now, I remember that I went to the flea market on Saturday from 7am until 3pm and then called harry so that I could go to his house. There I talked to him about multiple business ventures he plans, then we rode out, he showed me about 85% of his 80 acres and it was amazing to see. Riding on the tractor while he moved trees and went through the growth of the path was one of the most fun things I have done yet. I wish to be a part of the things he had planned, though I do not know if he truly has the energy and time.

I stayed there until about 7:15 then headed home. To do the things you have read about earlier.

Though on Saturday 10/27, I had a rough one and had to go to sleep early that night because of it. Well, I got up at 6 after going to sleep at three. I had a job to do with my present boss man. We had a job to do in Dawson. What I did was, because I love my mother and respect what she does. The night before I packed the truck to get it ready for the flea market, knowing that I had to get picked up. I dropped her off Friday night, to go drop off her items at the flea market so that she could have her place reserved. That's why I woke up at 6 because I need to be at the flea market at no later than 730 then at her job no later than 8. Once I dropped off her truck, Boss-man was ready to pick me up in the front of Wal-Mart, then we headed to Dawson. At Dawson, there are pictures on Facebook of the before. Boss-man made a schedule to finish at 12 though because I was the only one to tote the wheelbarrow and rake the leaves; the job went 2 hours over.

We finished and I was exhausted and seemed I was ready to cramp up, though it's good that I spaced out my water and food Consumption.

Now it's 10:30am and I didn't even realize Halloween was close because I try not to entertain the "craziness" much, though I have to work today and hopefully tomorrow. I remember seeing something on the T.V. in the wash house that law enforcement is going to crack down during Halloween, dealing with sex offenders, to keep the community safe, making sure that we are in a place where and when they say so. It's something to think about, though it is my life now, which brings up the reason I went to sleep so late on Friday night to the point I was looking at "porn" all day that day, off and on, since I found the phone. It's like I could not, or did not want to take myself away from the phone because of the reasons I placed above.

Surprisingly someone called me late that night after I placed some of my info on the web and said that she just felt that I was up, that felt weird and I thought and still think that she may have been on the same website. Knowing that I usually go to sleep early and wake up early, she still had "the feeling." We talked for a while about various things. However, one that stuck with me and is probably making this entry possible is that: she asked if my body will get out of the prison mode that I was in, and get me back to where I used to be. Note:

This female and I have been talking a lot lately about some deep stuff, not that I will go further than talking with her though that really got me back right. Going back to the things I use[d] to do and getting from what I have learned and/or attached to from prison. Exactly how I wrote it "….Went to sleep at 3 got up at 5…I can't go back to the same boy I was... I have to embrace and mold the other man I have discovered… Remind me of this when I get back… This connects too many things; the first is my openness. I was not open to many when I was out, Ms. Williams asked me was I ready and able to be open. I have told many that I was not afraid to be open with what I have going on and my past.

That's when she stated that unless I'm open people may not be interested in my story, it will not be legit. I have struggled with this previously because I saw that I had typed up some of my crazy thoughts before I went to prison, and wow I say wow again they were/crazy. When reading them, I felt the urge to erase them right then and try to forget about them. Though I knew I could not, so I did not. I was also thinking of just letting Ms. Williams read them then decide if I should publish them or not. Then all the above transpired and I realized that the boy I was in the past was weak-minded, childish, and petty. I could not accept to keep him hidden from the world to see the man I have become the strong-minded mature and relevant Lovely person he is. Though like I said the porn had a hold on me for about 12 hours straight, and I knew that it was a thing I had to censor though I was looking for the love that seems to be gone, yet I know it is always there. Understand that I am not nor was never addicted to porn, I binged when I get into it I do, though it was seldom. My thing was to always do my own thing to make my own memories of myself, being more meaningful to myself and my sexual partner. Though I see it was not because the Eros Love that was there was only the temporary as it explains and never grew into too much more. I'm going to stop there its 707 and I have to see what's planned for the day. Till next time

This is 1030am and it's been a long day, I had some ups and many downs, though I got through them and it's time to lay it down before 10, I'm hoping. I wish to make some money tomorrow because today has been like a water well that money flows freely. Now that I can start to make the moves that make the money needed to pay the occurring bills. But this is my final entry for this book is my goal for the present and future. "I have the ability to be great so why settle for mediocrity... I have the desire for a wife so why have a "girlfriend."

I am love so why would I settle for sex… O.N.E. Truth don't hurt nor hide so all that's required is that my eyes be open, my mind willing to accept and body ready to follow… LOVE SPREAD.

1/18/19

It's been some time since I have written it's now 1 18 2019 and this is my first time sitting down and putting thoughts together and the time to write from other things… many things have been happening and has happened… I went to Panama City, Tampa, Valdosta and many other places are up for grabs in my future…. I have been down in a very depressive stage, now I'm up and ready to go and look forward to the great things ahead. I have slacked on many different goals I had set before getting out, but they are still things that I wish and know that will be explored and dealt with. Writing, as you have noticed is not on the top priority of my mind though it is there in my mind. Especially being Facebook friends with Miss Williams; she makes sure the writing is haunting me knowing that I should do it. My cousin, Stacy, also stated to me about two days ago that writing will be my legacy to leave once I am gone and my empire to start.

Contact The Author

Maurice Harris

www.mauricesmileyharris.com

Maurice Harris is available for book talks, book signings, and speaking engagements.

Additional Resources

I have learned a lot about myself and situations that really impacted by childhood and teenage years and how many actions have impacted other people. A part of my personal growth has included learning more about sexual assault and its impact. It was helpful for me to talk with a victim of sexual assault. This really helped me understand how my actions may have affected the person I hurt.

The Additional Resources section of this book is here to provide information about the effects of abuse experienced by male victims and some research about sexual assault on college and university campuses. It also includes my conversation with a rape victim.

There is a lot of information available, right at our fingertips, but still so inaccessible in so many ways. It is my hope that this information can help someone else like it did me.

SIDELINED

A Conversation I Had With a
High School Classmate Who Was a Rape Victim

Victim: I just want to know because we were talking around that time…I'm lost because I know you had no reason to rape anyone.

Me: In 2010, my football career ended. I was a womanizer already, but I became a coward that could not hide behind football pads. I blamed everyone else but myself for my failures. I was then in an already destructive relationship, and once it got tough and I thought it was over between me and the girl, I took advantage of her, attempting to release all of my pain on her. Which as you can guess, the pain became worse. I added that relationship to something else I failed at.

Victim: I always knew you had a couple of loose screws…I never saw you doing anything like that. Is there something that's called rape in a relationship? Well, I have a few questions. And I'm only because I'm also a rape victim, but I was able to forgive and move forward. What was going on in your mind? Like, what were you thinking? I'm only asking because you realize you made a mistake and you were out of character, which means you are trying to forgive yourself for it and move on.

Me: I wasn't thinking, just acting…I was trying to think less as possible. I know it is rape…I apologize about what happened to you…I apologize for opening the wound back up…I felt as though I owed me sex when I wanted it. I made excuses for why it was right.

Victim: Most guys think like that so it's not just you…you get what I'm saying? Most girls put up with it. I think a lot of guys release their pain through sex…where do you think rough sex comes from? You didn't open a wound it was just something I've been waiting to ask you. To be real, I've been asking everyone about you and only one person actually kept it real and has your back. I was just scared of what you were going to say.

Me: Scared of what I was going to say…how?

Victim: It wasn't right but, most guys like that…know to ask what happened. People involved in rape culture just don't talk about it.

Me: You're right about the culture…it sucks! I agree…you're totally correct.

Victim: You have a bigger purpose that's why you went through that. It could have been worse, you could have got more time. Let go of the pain and capitalize from it. It's your story, your life, move forward. I meant now capitalize from it. It doesn't just stop with you…now it's time for you to educate others since you are bouncing back from the loss. I have seen you make plenty of steps forward, now it's time for you to educate someone else about your situation.

Common Effects of Abuse Experienced by
Male Victims

To be clear, if a victim of child sexual abuse experiences arousal or physical pleasure during the abuse, that does not mean the victim is consenting. It is still an act of abuse against a child.

- Experiencing mental health issues such as anxiety or depression
- Questioning sexual orientation

- Fearing a shortened future

- Feeling a loss of masculinity

- Unable to relax

- Avoiding recollection of the abuse or assault

- Trouble sleeping

- Withdrawing from relationships

- Fearing judgment or disbelief if someone finds out about the abuse

On the path of healing, it is important that male victims recognize they are not alone. At least 1 in 6 men have been sexually abused or assaulted in their lifetime.

Source: Behavioral Sciences Online Journal www.mdpi.com

Male Victims of Child Sexual Abuse

RAINN

According to the Rape, Abuse & Incest National Network (RAINN), male victims of child sexual abuse may feel additional shame, guilt, or self-doubt. They may blame themselves for being "too weak" to stop the abuse or attack.

Source: Abuselawsuit.com

Long-term psychological effects:

- Depression
- Post-traumatic stress disorder (PTSD)
- Anxiety
- Low self-esteem or self-image
- Cognitive impairment
- Eating disorders
- Increased risk of substance abuse
- Increased risk of unsafe sexual behaviors
- Increased risk of self-harm
- Increased risk of suicide
- Relationship problems (including intimacy issues in future relationships)

However, boys or men who were victims of sexual violence may experience additional consequences based on society's stereotypes around masculinity. Although girls are more likely to be sexually abused, 1 in 13 boys experience sexual abuse before reaching 18 years of age.

A Brief Report of Sexual Violence among Universities with NCAA Division I Athletic Programs
Jacquelyn D. Wiersma- Mosley and Kristen N. Jozkowski

Violence against women on college campuses continues to be a pervasive public health problem with approximately one in five women experiencing sexual assault and one in nine women experiencing rape while in college. The current study examined relationship and sexual violence among National Collegiate Athletic Association (NCAA) Division I universities. Based on previous research, Division I universities seem to report higher rates of sexual assault, but within-group differences have yet to be examined. The data include 1,422 four-year private and public institutions with at least 1,000 students who submitted Clery data (2014) on rape, domestic and dating violence, and stalking. Division I campuses reported significantly higher reports of violence against women compared to Division II, III, and universities with no athletic programs

"We masked our troubles with sex which allowed us to feel accepted by the other and avoid getting to know each other beyond small talk and sex. The "good" in the relationship slowly dissipated and became toxic –explosive if you will. The constant breaking up and getting back together became a pattern. It was the 'mentally troubled' part that kept bringing us back to each other knowing it was unhealthy. I had an immature mind and didn't want to fully walk away and start anew. Covering up and ignoring things about people or myself became my normal in relationships".

On average, athletes are more likely than other students on

campus to identify with hyper-masculinity and to accept "rape myths" to justify sexual assaults. Evidence also suggests they're more likely to be confused about consent and admit to having committed acts of sexual aggression.

OTL: College athletes three times more likely to be named in Title IX sexual misconduct complaints
Paula Lavigne, Nov 2018

COLLEGE ATHLETES IN recent years were about three times more likely than other students to be accused of sexual misconduct or domestic violence in complaints made at Power 5 conference schools, according to an analysis by Outside the Lines.

That finding is based upon data from Title IX complaints covering allegations of sexual assault, domestic violence, sexual exploitation, sexual coercion, stalking or retaliation collected from 32 Power 5 schools that provided records in response to requests for complaints against athletes over the past six years. Outside the Lines sought the data from all 65 Power 5 schools, but some officials did not provide information, and some that did provide information did not do so for all years.

The data provided show that, on average, about 6.3 percent of Title IX complaints against students - whether the complaint resulted in a formal investigation or not - included an athlete as the person accused of wrongdoing, officially called a "respondent" in the reports. Though that percentage equates to a minority of the overall number of complaints at Power 5 campuses made during the time period, athletes were named in such reports more often than might be expected considering they represent, on average, just

1.7 percent of total student enrollment at the universities.

Works Cited

247 Sports. (n.d.) Maurice Harris.
https://247sports.com/Player/Maurice-Harris-
52764/?PlayerInstitution=90179

Behavioral Sciences Online Journal. Common effects of Abuse
Experienced by Male Victims. https://www.mdpi.com

Coley Harvey and Orlando Sentinel. "Former Florida State
Linebacker Maurice Harris charged with sexual assault.
Orlando Sentinel Newspaper, 9 May, 2011,
https://www.dc.state.fl.us

Florida. "District Court of Appeal." First District of Florida, 16
Dec 2021, https://www.1dca.org

Lavigne, Paula. Nov 2018. OTL: College athletes three times
more likely to be named in Title IX sexual misconduct
complaints.
ESPN.https://www.espn.com/espn/otl/story/_/id/2514925
9/college-athletes-three-s-more-likely-named-title-ix-
sexual-misconduct-complaints

Orlando Sentinel. 2011, May 8. Former Florida State LB
Maurice Harris charged with sexual assault.
https://www.orlandosentinel.com/sports/os-xpm-2011-
05-09-os-maurice-harris-rape-0510-20110509-story.html

Wiersma- Mosley, Jacquelyn D., and Jozkowski, Kristen N. "A
    Brief Report of Sexual Violence among Universities with
    NCAA Division I Athletic Programs." Behavioral
    Sciences, Feb. 2019, v9(2).

    https://www.ncbi.nlm.nih.gov/pmc/articles/PMC6406521
    /www.ncaa.org

Photo Credits

247SPORTS
Seminoles.com
Cameon Meller/NoleDigest.com